Inner Cleansing

LIVING CLEAN IN A POLLUTED WORLD

Nancy Corbett

PRISM · UNITY

Published in Great Britain 1993 by
PRISM PRESS
2 South Street
Bridport
Dorset DT6 3NQ

Originally published in Australia by
SALLY MILNER PUBLISHING
558 Darling Street
Rozelle NSW 2039

ISBN 1 85327 083 0

© Write-On Publishing Pty Ltd, 1993

Printed by The Guernsey Press Ltd, The Channel Islands.

Cover:
The Idler
Janet Cumbrae Stewart
Pastel on paper
Purchased 1922
Collection of the Queensland Art Gallery

Contents

INTRODUCTORY

1   *There's Something We Can Do*

'If you want to change the world, start small.'

Peace Corps advertisement

This book is about the process of inner cleansing: how it works and why it's so effective in countering the toxins stored in your cells after years of exposure to chemical additives and other ubiquitous poisons. It's about how cleansing can help you not only to avoid disease, but to enjoy exuberant vitality and real wellness.

It is written in response to the steadily worsening conditions for our health in the chemical society we've created since approximately 1945. It is not an evangelistic, bullying book. It won't support any feelings of either guilt or helplessness you may have in the face of the barrage of undeniably bad news about the air you breathe, the water you drink and the food you eat.

The reason for this is simply that although it's true that we are all being exposed to unprecendented attacks on our health, vitality and common sense, it's not true that there's nothing we can do about it.

There *is* something we can do. It's uncomplicated, effective, and creates optimum conditions for our own well-being. We don't have to live in a polluted world. Inside and out, we can create the conditions for our own good health. We can do it for ourselves, and we can do it by ourselves.

We are the unwitting targets of thousands of substances which our bodies, the miraculous result of many thousands of years of slow adaptation to a slowly changing environment, were never designed to process. Every day we breathe, drink and eat a multitude of substances created in the laboratories of the Western world, substances which did not even exist on the planet until a few years ago. None of them have been tested over a long period of time; none of them have been tested for safety in combination with each other. The experiment in how they can harm us has just begun. We are the subjects of the experiment; we are its guinea pigs. But we don't have to be its victims.

Knowledge is power

Knowledge is power, and the information in *Inner Cleansing* can give you the power effectively to combat the things which may be injurious to your health.

Perhaps you think it's too late. Perhaps you already suffer from some chronic disease such as asthma or hypertension. Or you're not exactly ill, but you're not exactly well, either. You may lack energy and frequently feel exhausted; you may experience sudden mood swings, emotional outbursts, depression, vague aches and pains, odd skin eruptions or restless sleep. You may be overweight, having tried various diets to lose weight without much success. You may suffer allergic reactions of various kinds, often hard to pinpoint because they're masked, but resulting in numerous unpleasant symptoms.

In fact, you may not have felt *really* well for years. And you may have become resigned to these symptoms, accepting them as an inevitable part of your

genetic heritage, or of growing older. **They're not.**
And the simple cleansing processes described in this
book can make an enormous difference to any and
all of them.

Or you may think it's too early. You feel all right,
you look after yourself, you're still young. Good! By
understanding and using the information presented
here, you can continue to feel well. You can avoid
the otherwise inevitable accumulation of toxins in
your body which may eventually lower your vitality
and attack your immune system, leading to the symptoms described above, or any of a host of equally
disagreeable other ones.

Your body is not a machine composed of mysterious and potentially dangerous parts and processes
which may inexplicably break down or attack you.
It is, in fact, your best friend; a beautifully functioning whole; an organic, integrated system capable of
healing and balancing itself even under the most adverse conditions.

There are, however, many things which interfere
with its ability to regulate and harmonise itself. This
is amply proven by the devastating increase in the
incidence of the so-called 'lifestyle' diseases — heart
disease, cancer, arthritis, diabetes, high blood pressure — which have supplanted bacterial epidemics
such as cholera, typhoid and tuberculosis as the main
killers in the industrialised societies of the world.
All of these diseases result, generally speaking, from
conditions over which you have a significant measure of control. If you smoke; if you take drugs
designed to suppress the symptoms of your body's
struggle to heal itself; if you eat the typical Western
diet loaded with fats, salt, sugar and relentlessly

'processed' and chemicalised foods; if you do nothing to help yourself counteract the stresses of living in a noisy, dirty, fast-paced and competitive social environment, then your body, while doing its best for as long as it possibly can, may eventually become exhausted and fail to cope.

Even if you already practise healthier habits than these, a clear awareness of the hidden dangers in the contemporary environment and a corresponding understanding of the process of natural cleansing will give you the best possible foundation for working *with* your own inner healer. You will have the power, based on knowledge, to counteract the negative factors of modern life. You can take the initiative and establish the optimum conditions for maintaining the good health and energy which will allow your life to develop into a wonderful fulfilment of all its creative possibilities, and not into a trial of disease, difficulty and regret about the things you could have done, but didn't, because your resources were used up in the struggle simply to survive.

We're living today in a complex, sophisticated world. We may sometimes feel overwhelmed by the sheer volume of information from many different sources, and from conflicting advice issuing from a multitude of specialists and experts. By understanding some basic principles, however, we can benefit from the undeniably impressive discoveries of the age, and put its abundance of knowledge to good use in our lives. As Louis Pauwels and Jacques Bergier advised in their book *Morning of the Magicians*, 'Let everything be reported. Then one day we may have a revelation.' It's time for that revelation.

With a solid foundation of understanding our own

process of inner healing and how it works to combat the stresses and toxins it encounters, we can move from a position of confusion and passivity to one of power. We can take what we need from the world around us, use it to our very best advantage, and let the rest go by.

2   *Healing Ourselves*

*'There seems no plan because it is all plan; there
seems no centre because it is all centre.'*

C.S. Lewis

Your body is not a machine composed of various parts
but an amazingly complex single organism. All its
aspects and processes are interrelated. The state of
health, too, is a single thing, both affecting and
affected by every facet of the self.

Your body is, in fact, a miracle of self-maintenance
and self-healing. It heals itself or it doesn't get healed
at all. Of course, beneficial conditions can be provided for the healing that takes place naturally. When
you cut your finger, for example, you can help the
healing process by keeping the injured area clean
and free as far as possible from bacteria that could
exacerbate the injury. But the actual response of the
body — the mobilisation of the immune system, the
production of new cells and tissue to mend the
damage — is a self-generated one, and nothing else
can initiate it.

We've all been influenced by the traditions of our
culture, and one of the most fundamental of these
is the belief that 'experts' in a particular field know
best. In the matter of health, for the past few centuries those experts have been doctors. Many of us still
believe that doctors know more about our health than
we do. While it's certainly true that a doctor's
knowledge of disease is much greater than that of

the average layperson, we can and should take more responsibility for our own health needs.

Hippocrates, long acknowledged as the father of Western medicine, would scarcely recognise it today. It's doubtful whether this man, who based his teachings on the idea that the body can only be understood as a whole, would approve of the recent medical trend toward increased specialisation, or its 'spare parts', high-tech focus. His writings emphasise that in no way can the suppression of disease symptoms equal successful treatment.

Hippocrates was born in 460 BC on the Greek island of Cos. His careful observation, rational conclusions and supremely ethical approach to healing are as relevant today as they were then. The school of medicine which he founded on Cos believed in a moderate diet, cleanliness and rest when a person was ill or wounded. They though that the physician should interfere **as little as possible** with the healing processes of Nature. They emphasised that it was better to prevent disease, if possible, than to have to try to cure it.

Many of Hippocrates' sayings, such as 'One man's meat is another man's poison' and 'Let food be your medicine and medicine your food' are part of our general folklore. And he expressed a humble common sense which sometimes seems to have been forgotten by the medical profession.

Other particularly relevant sayings of Hippocrates include:

'Do not hesitate to ask the opinion of laymen, if any improvement in treatment may result in doing so', and

> 'Healing is a matter of time, but sometimes also a matter of opportunity. Hence medical practice must not depend primarily on plausible theories, but instead on experience combined with reason',

and

> 'Care for the sick and make them well, care for the healthy to keep them well, and care for yourself'.

The growing contemporary movement in holistic medicine represents a welcome return to the Hippocratic tradition. Holism is simply the recognition that **the whole is greater than the sum of its parts.** Holistic healing methods are based on an awareness that the body is a unified entity — mental, physical and spiritual — and must be acknowledged as such by anyone seeking to aid the healing process.

Similarly, health is not simply the absence of pain or disease but the condition of being **well** in body, mind and spirit. Joy, balance, peace of mind and creative energy are integral elements of real well being.

We can create our own good health

Each of us has the power and the potential to create our own good health. No-one else can do it for us. This is good news indeed, as is the fact that our own healing potential is an immense and deeply wise resource. Most therapeutic treatments are limited to alleviating symptoms or improving the basic conditions in which our healing can progress; they don't cure the underlying condition which is causing the symptoms. Our bodies do that.

The most essential part of this process is the body's

ability to cleanse itself of substances which are injurious to it. This cleansing takes place *automatically* whenever there is enough energy left over from the demands of muscular exertion, digestion and all the other 'housekeeping' functions required of the body on a daily basis.

When we rest, when we sleep, when we reduce the large amount of body energy needed to digest heavy food, the amount of cleansing which can occur increases dramatically. A lot of vitality is required to run a human being! When you rest, your body immediately and efficiently uses the extra vitality at its disposal to get rid of accumulated toxins and other wastes, and to heal and repair damaged tissues.

It's a natural biological process. It goes on all the time. It works. And if your sleep is always regular and restful, if you've never been exposed to chemicals in your air or water, if you eat nothing but organic foods, if you have a strong genetic heritage and have never suffered any stress, then you probably need think no more about it. You're also not living on planet Earth in the final years of the twentieth century! It's a sad fact that even the penguins in the remote Antarctic have residues of DDT and other poisons in their cells these days.

Certainly it's important to eat the best possible food, avoid obvious poisons and take steps to handle high levels of stress. The healthier your basic lifestyle is, the more efficiently your body will eliminate waste products and accumulated chemicals, and the better your immune system will work to protect you.

But in addition to these sensible fundamentals, you can give yourself enormous extra help by giving your body more of the rest it needs to carry out its cleansing and healing functions. **The most effective way to do this is simply to cut down on the amount of energy required to digest food.**

Resting the body

Abstaining from concentrated foods for short periods of time is a way of greatly extending the rest needed by the body to combat the build-up of wastes and chemicals from the environment, from medications, and from bacteria. A tired body or one which is working flat out to keep you functioning will, in time, become overburdened and less efficient at cleansing itself. When this happens, the immune system, overwhelmed by having to deal with chemicals and pollutants of all kinds, is suppressed, and its ability to cope with infection and disease is reduced.

One of the first signs of an illness is loss of appetite. Conversely, the return of appetite is a clear signal that we're well on the mend. There's an excellent reason for this. The body knows exactly what it needs in a crisis. It needs to turn its resources to healing. It needs you to stop diverting those resources to digesting unnecessary food for a while.

A sick dog or cat stops eating, too. It doesn't force itself to eat because it thinks it "should keep its strength up". No-one can make it take the food its instincts tell it to avoid. But we may be programmed to override our own common sense and body wisdom. We feel we should eat something, even if we have to force it down, and that failing to do so will slow down our recovery. Nothing could be further from the truth.

Every one of the body's innumerable cells depends on two main processes to sustain life. It must absorb nourishment, and it must get rid of the wastes that accumulate during the chemical changes which occur within the cell while it is absorbing that nourishment. The complementary balancing of these two processes, the dynamic equilibrium of a healthy cell (or a healthy body) is called *homeostasis*. If this balance is upset, the cell can't function properly.

If the energy of the cell has to be used to deal with a relentless input of food at the same time that it's trying to dispose of excess waste, its functioning is seriously impaired. The waste continues to accumulate. The cell becomes more and more overwhelmed by its own toxicity. But if the supply of food is stopped for a while, the cell can concentrate on eliminating the toxins. It can heal itself and restore its proper balance. Once it does so, it will be able to benefit again from nourishment.

As with the cell, so with the body as a whole. If we eat too much, or eat when our body needs rest in order to carry out its healing function efficiently, the ability to eliminate unwanted substances of all kinds is seriously affected. Large amounts of toxic matter may accumulate and we could literally poison ourselves. Retained toxins, stored in various parts of the body, can manifest as chronic diseases such as nephritis (if they're stored in the kidney tissue) or fibrositis (if stored in the muscles).

So, whenever the body is given a chance, it goes into its house cleaning mode. It takes every possible opportunity to cleanse and heal itself. If you rest — especially by cutting down on digestion and physical exercise — there's much more energy than usual available for this task. Energy can be deployed in different ways. And in the case of your body's process- es, this suddenly available energy will be used for the body's inner work of cleansing, detoxification and healing at the cellular level.

The benefits of self-cleansing

Going onto a light diet, or even just juices or water for a few days, allows the body to devote much more energy than usual to self-cleansing, repair of damaged tissues and general healing.

In its wisdom, the body doesn't turn to the mus- cles or organs when it requires energy for its process- es during a fast. It turns mainly to its reserves of fat, where the majority of wastes are stored, and by the process of *autolysis**, or self-digestion, breaks down the fats, makes use of their stored energy, and eliminates the stored wastes.

*The metabolism of fasting is characterised by two processes. One is called *gluconeogenesis*, which is the body's means of maintaining normal blood sugar levels. When little or no food is taken in, the body mobilises stored energy sources, primarily glycogen and fat, to maintain adequate blood sugar levels. Small amounts of protein are utilised but this is not significant as far as total pro- tein stores are concerned. The body will not expend its important proteins when it can use fat as an alternative, less valuable energy source. Thus fat, which is not neces- sary for ongoing metabolic processes, as is protein, is the primary energy source during a fast.

Autolysis, on the other hand, is a process whereby any sort of excess substance in the tissues is broken down through cellular enzyme activity to provide other sources

During autolysis, damaged cells can be eliminated or repaired, and the whole process of energy absorption and waste elimination becomes more efficient. It's a bit like what happens when you clean the carburettor of your car; the fuel burns more cleanly and there's more energy at your disposal.

Another beneficial effect of this process is that the elimination of dead or dying cells, and the development and growth of new ones, are both accelerated by the cleansing process. Since one of the factors in physical aging is that the cells are breaking down at a faster rate than they are being replaced, it follows that a process which helps to tip the balance in the other direction is a rejuvenating one.

The first cells to be consumed by the body during a fast are usually the very ones you'll be happy to get rid of. Tissues tend to be broken down in the reverse order of their usefulness. Diseased or damaged tissues, abcesses, benign tumours, and excess fat are sometimes the first to go. Your body knows what it's doing and will do it very efficiently, if given the chance.

Perhaps even more surpising than the efficiency with which the body burns up the material it will benefit most from eliminating is the fact that, dur-

of nourishment during a fast. These substances include various metabolic by-products such as cholesterol, excess acids, and proteolytic metabolites. These are broken down and eliminated through the various organs of elimination during a fast.

Gluconeogenesis may be included under the broad heading of autolysis but strictly speaking they are separate, simultaneous processes.

ing a time of eating lightly, the proteins needed for the development of new cells continue to be produced. Proteins, or rather the amino acids from which they are built, can be synthesised constantly by the body from the very cells which are being decomposed in the process of autolysis. In spite of the fact that no protein is being eaten, the serum albumin reading (which is a measure of the protein level in your blood) stays constant during even a prolonged period without food.

Taking little or no food at times is a very widespread phenomenon in the natural world, and not only in sick animals. A bear fasts all through the northern winter, conserving its energy for warmth during the long months when food is scarce. Many birds don't eat for weeks while sitting on their eggs. Animals often fast during their mating season, and even while nursing their young. And both animals and people go without food, with no ill effects, as a survival mechanism during periods of scarcity.

Cutting back on food consumption doesn't just occur as an instinctive procedure when we are ill, of course, or as a result of unavoidable food scarcity following some disaster. Throughout recorded history, people all over the world have voluntarily fasted to increase their spiritual well-being and clarity of mind or to focus public attention on what they perceived to be an injustice. Jesus commenced his ministry by going without food for forty days and nights in the desert; Gandhi took only water at times in order to draw the eyes of the world to India's oppression by colonial rule; feminists refused food early in the century to demonstrate the sincerity of their commitment to achieving democratic rights for women. Short periods of abstinence from heavy foods are an integral part of the religious practice of millions of Hindus and Buddhists.

The practice is commonly used as a preparation for initiation ceremonies by many indigenous peoples, and it's considered essential to the cultivation of extraordinary mental powers by shamans and tribal healers. In all these varied contexts, it is clearly recognised as a process which, far from weakening its practitioners, gives them greater power.

'OK. The next time I get sick, I'll cut out food for a couple of days.'

Excellent idea.

'What if I cut out food for a while when I'm not sick?'

Another excellent idea.

Resting and its adjunct, cutting down on the consumption of food, help immeasurably in the alleviation of many chronic and acute diseases. But by increasing your body's opportunities to cleanse itself while you are still in relatively good health, you can also increase your vitality, strengthen your immune system and help prevent disease in the first place.

You'll enjoy a wonderful range of benefits if you make the simple cleansing process a regular part of your life. You'll feel better and look better. Your eyes and skin will be clearer; so will your mind. Your concentration will improve. Your digestion will be better, and with your newly-cleaned tastebuds, food will taste fantastic. All your senses, in fact, will be sharpened. Your metabolism will function more efficiently and, as more oxygen is delivered to your cells, you'll feel more fit. Your joints will be more flexible. You'll lose weight, if you want to. You'll have more energy and endurance than before. You'll feel calmer, more centred in yourself, more emotionally and psychologically balanced. And you'll be using your mind to help your body keep you healthy in the most practical possible way.

Before outlining the different cleansing programmes, however, let's turn our attention to some of the factors that make cleansing so necessary as a health practice today.

3 Concepts of Health and Disease

'In the West, our desire to conquer Nature often means simply that we diminish the probability of small inconveniences at the cost of increasing the probability of very large disasters.'

Kenneth E. Boulding

We live in challenging times. The concepts underlying the explosion of scientific knowledge in the last three centuries are in a process of enormous change and reappraisal. But it always takes a long time for the theories and discoveries at the leading edge of human thought to filter through to the level of practice, and nowhere is this more obvious — or more important to you — than in the field of medicine.

Before moving on to look at some of the new ideas, it's useful to have a clear understanding of past elements which have created our present concepts of health and disease. A solid understanding of where we've come from enables us to make more informed choices about the future.

Throughout most of human history, disease has been regarded as one manifestation of the spiritual aspect of a person's life, and healers have been regarded (and still are) as having supernatural powers. Their role has been to act as mediums between the world of everyday reality and the unknown world where the disease originated. Whether this world is one of malevolent spirits or the source of microscopic substances such as viruses and bacteria (often equally obscure to the layman) makes little difference to the sufferer. And in both cases, those people who believe in the healer's special powers over the frightening unknown tend to recover more often, and more quickly, than those who have little faith in the person they've called on for help.

Healing and our belief system

But surely modern medicine, with its dazzling technology, its rigorous testing methods and insistence on 'objective' standards and attitudes, is a far cry from the practices of shamans, witchdoctors and medicine men and women? Certainly it is, in some important ways, but the basic fact of healing has never changed. We heal ourselves, sometimes with the help of modern medical skills, and sometimes in spite of them. And a key factor in our healing is our own belief system; what we think about the nature of disease, what we perceive our responsibility for it to be, and how we view the interventions of the healer. In these respects we are exactly the same as any more primitive human being faced with the same situation.

Copernicus, Galileo and Bacon

The main strands of the mass belief system which has resulted in our present highly developed industrial society began to emerge about five centuries ago, when Nicolas Copernicus challenged the accepted Ptolemaic view that planet Earth was the centre of the Universe. Copernicus suspected that Earth was one of a number of planets circling around a smallish star somewhere in the outer fringes of a relatively limited galaxy in an unimaginably vast system. He had the good sense to keep this radical idea to himself, and delayed making his notions public until the year of his death.

Galileo's observations with a wonderful new toy called a telescope supported Copernicus' theory beyond any doubt, but Galileo was less cautious about communicating his findings — and paid the price for it. The established order was not at all impressed with an idea which shattered the foundations of its own beliefs.

Nevertheless, truth and knowledge are hard things to suppress in the world of curious human beings, and Galileo's empirical approach, and his carefully-documented observations, not only formed the basis of scientific progress in the seventeenth century but are still influential today.

It was Galileo's view that scientists should restrict their conclusions about the nature of reality to what could be measured objectively. It's not difficult to see why he considered this necessary, given the stranglehold of superstition and vested interests of the society in which he lived. This new scientific objectivity had a profound effect on increasing knowledge, and has undoubtedly influenced our world more in the past four hundred years than any other single factor.

Culture-shattering ideas never occur in isolation. Ideas whose time has come invariably appear spontaneously in more than one mind and in more than one place. This is true of the theory of evolution, for example, and of the germ theory of disease. It was true of Galileo's intuition of the importance of building a body of knowledge on quantifiable foundations. At the same time as he was carrying out his experiments in Italy, Francis Bacon was doing the same in England.

Bacon was a tireless and persuasive advocate of this new method of inductive learning. Knowledge was to be based on experiments which could be repeated, and therefore verified, by anyone following the same procedures. The conclusions to be drawn from them were the property of anyone who cared enough about the truth to go to the trouble of testing it.

Unfortunately, Bacon threw out the baby with the bathwater. In his passionate rejection of the older notions of an integrated natural order which included the realms of spirit and intuition as well as measurable facts, an essential balance was lost. We are only beginning to regain it now.

In his thorough (and thoroughly inspiring) book on the great changes now taking place in contemporary thought, called *The Turning Point: Science, Society and the Rising Culture*, the physicist Fritjof Capra notes that Bacon not only specifically dismissed the perception of the earth as a nurturing mother, but expressed his ideas of how she was to be approached in the idiom of the shamefully widespread witch trials of his time. In fact, as attorney-general for King James I, Bacon had a considerable amount to do with witch trials. He seems to have applied his ideas from one area of interest to the other. Nature, he wrote, was to be 'hounded in her wanderings' and 'made a slave', while the scientist's role was 'to torture nature's secrets from her'. Nature had always been regarded as female and it seems no accident that some of the new sense of power felt by the rising rank of scientists contained an element of gloating. At last, it seemed, man could achieve a measure of control over what had always seemed to be dangerously erratic and mysterious.

The shift in thinking which resulted from the work of Galileo, Bacon and others was essentially a shift from an organic, unified view of reality, usually religious in nature, to the image of the world as a machine. This shift was immeasurably strengthened by the influence of two other cultural giants, Descartes and Newton.

Living beings as machines

It was Descartes who said 'Cogito, ergo sum'. By the identification of our entire being with the brain, and specifically its capacity for rational thought, Descartes' teachings greatly increased the propensity in Western philosophy to regard mind and body as separate from each other. Not only were human beings seen as divided from the rest of the natural world (as they always had been, in Christian teaching) but now the split extended right into the self.

In the Cartesian view of nature, the entire universe is a mechanical system composed of a multitude of separate objects. It was a short jump from this to the idea that living beings — plants, animals and human beings — were also, essentially, machines. The way to understand how a machine works is to reduce it to its basic elements and functions. This philosophy, called reductionism, still forms the basis of much of our scientific and medical education today.

Isaac Newton, a mathematician, looked at the empirical, inductive method of scientific exploration proposed by Bacon and the rational, deductive method proposed by Descartes. In his view, both elements were necessary. Experimentation alone was not enough; its results required systematic interpretation. Deduction from first principles was not enough, either; experimental evidence was needed to back it up. In his revolutionary book, *Principia Mathematica*, published in 1687, he brought the two approaches together and, in doing so, established the scientific method we've used in the West ever since.

Classical physics (and all the other sciences, because they base their methodology on that of physics) is founded on the scientific methods of Bacon, the philosophy of Descartes, and the mathematical theory of Newton. Matter was seen as the basis of existence, and the material world as a multitude of separate objects forming a great 'world-machine'. The machine, no matter how complex, could be understood by reducing it to its basic building blocks, and examining the ways in which they interacted with each other.

The fact that this way of approaching reality works better when studying inanimate objects than living systems has not stopped it from being applied as inflexibly to biology as to other sciences. One of the results of this is that our knowledge of biology, vast as it is in terms of interesting facts about all sorts of things, is seriously lacking when it comes to comprehending the function of living systems **as a whole**. The interactions which occur within any living being, and the relationship between a living entity and its environment are far from clearly understood. Much of our present ecological dilemma is a direct result of this lack of insight, as well as the entrenched attitude of scientists that Nature is an enemy which must be defeated before she defeats us. In some ways our ancestors, lacking both the advantages and the limitations of a rigorously-defined scientific method, possessed far greater wisdom about how things actually work.

The reductionist, mechanistic scientific approach has been spectacularly successful in creating a sophisticated technology. Its obvious success explains why it has seldom been questioned until now. We can manipulate natural forces with astounding and often beneficial results. The productivity of human labour has been immeasurably increased by the industrialised processes stemming from the scientific discoveries made over the past three centuries. Life in the developed countries has attained a degree of ease and even luxury for many, many people. But now, in the final years of the twentieth century, the limitations of the approach are becoming disturbingly evident.

4   *A New Direction in Medicine*

'If we can combine our knowledge of science with the wisdom of wildness...our potentialities appear to be unbounded.'

Charles Lindbergh

Nowhere are both the advantages and limitations of the scientific method more obvious than in the practice of medicine. Nowhere have its successes and failures been so dramatic.

By the beginning of the century the structure of the body had been studied in minute detail and medical researchers were looking further and deeper for the causes of disease. When Louis Pasteur established a clear correlation between the presence of certain microscopic organisms called bacteria and the incidence of specific illnesses (and his theories were given strong immediate support by the outbreak of a series of bacteria-caused epidemics in Europe at the time) it appeared a perfect explanation and one which fitted well within the framework of nineteenth century scientific belief. Any lingering notion that disease might be the result of a complex interplay of environmental factors, both internal and external, was dismissed in the light of the germ theory of disease.

Certain disease states could now be explained as the direct results of specific attacks by specific microbes. It was extremely neat, comfortingly in tune with the mechanistic view of matter, and true enough, as far as it went, to be persuasive.

When continued research led to the development of effective vaccines against infectious diseases such as typhoid, tetanus, smallpox and diptheria, the germ theory of disease seemed not only to be proven beyond a doubt but to be the most fruitful model for medical advances in other areas, too.

No denigration of Pasteur's work, or that of the medical researchers who followed him, is intended. Any reader over forty years old will remember the fully justified fear of parents every summer when there was an outbreak of polio, for example. Our present reprieve from many fatal or disabling illnesses is no small thing. Not least among Pasteur's many contributions was the fact that his discoveries led to the practice of antiseptic conditions in surgery, saving numerous lives once lost because of post-surgical infections.

But Pasteur himself had a broader view of the relationship between the development of a disease and the inner environment of the person afflicted by it than did many of his followers. He was well aware of the fact that only *some* of the people exposed to any disease-causing bacteria actually got sick, and he was interested in why this was so. He assumed, correctly, that if the body was in balance it could mount a successful resistance to the same bacteria that might kill another person living in the same conditions. He knew too that every body, healthy or not, always harbours a wide variety of bacteria and that the mere presence of even a dangerous strain was not a complete answer to the question of why people got sick.

Finding the cause of every illness

The success of the germ theory in explaining disease, however, was so much in tune with the prevailing Cartesian methods and ideas that this broader perspective was swamped in the ensuing fervour to find the specific cause of every illness. The discovery of penicillin in 1928 further strengthened the belief that the way to defeat disease was to find the particular substance that was causing it, and then the particular substance, 'the magic bullet', which would home in on the offender and destroy it, leaving the rest of the organism intact.

The era of the wonder-drugs further convinced the general public, including doctors, that there must be a specific drug cure for almost everything. The enormous success of antibiotics led to a widely held conviction that doctors and scientists were experts who could and would eventually discover the cause and cure of every disease. So impressive had medicine been in dealing with infectious diseases that a vast public expectation was created: the hero-doctor could, and should, be able to cure anything. The age-old war against illness was nearly over, and doctors were the officers in the winning army.

As every new avenue of medical expertise developed, the same reductionist principles were applied. For example, the conventional belief that mind and body were somehow separate from each other led to the placing of mental disorders in a different category from physical illness. Although a great gulf existed, therefore, between the work of psychiatrists and other doctors, psychiatry tried to prove that it, too, was a 'real' science by adhering rigorously to the biomedical model.

As a result, mental illness has primarily been studied in terms of a disruption of the normal physical functioning of the brain. Although this is no doubt true in some cases, the narrowness of focus resulted, until recently, in a serious lack of understanding of the role of stress and the emotions in both mental and ostensibly 'physical' illnesses. Like their colleagues who treat the body, the doctors dealing with the mind looked mainly to physical or chemical intervention for a cure.

In both areas of medical practice, the consistent trend has been toward increased specialisation, to becoming more and more reductionist, to looking at smaller and smaller 'units' of the body in an effort to pinpoint where the trouble was coming from, and where to intervene to fix it. The large picture, the awareness that a person is a dynamic, integrated being whose own inner balance has a great deal to do with his or her overall health, is only now starting to gain widespread support among the doctors who are part of the growing holistic health movement.

Belief in the medical profession's omnipotence

Until very recently, however, holistic practitioners were widely dismissed by the rest of the medical profession as charlatans. As medicine became more and more complex; as surgical procedures became increasingly sophisticated; as our magazines and television shows repeatedly astounded us with the many miracles of modern medicine; as an arsenal of new drugs was developed and used, often successfully, to treat the symptoms of every imaginable condition; so the popular belief in the omnipotence of doctors continued to grow. With their specialised training, only they seemed to have the expertise to know what should be done when we were sick. We came to expect a cure, or some sort of medical intervention (usually in the form or a drug or surgery) for everything from the natural processes of birth and death to our feelings of sadness when we lost someone we loved.

The doctors themselves fostered this unhealthy state of affairs by jealously guarding their position as the only people qualified to deal with illness in any of its forms. Medicine is a prestigious and well paid profession, and it would be naive to assume that doctors have never entered it for these reasons. It is a conservative profession, slow to accept changes. While this is good in some ways, it can create a situation where a powerful social group acts to reinforce a status quo which is not always in our best interests.

One startling example of how this has affected the practice of contemporary medicine can be seen in the Flexner Report of 1910. As described by Harvey and Marilyn Diamond in their book *Living Health*, a man named Alexander Flexner was appointed in 1909 by the Carnegie Foundation to visit every institution in America which provided training in health care. The purpose of his survey was to recommend to the Carnegie and Rockefeller Foundations which schools should be funded by grants.

It may not be entirely a coincidence that only those schools which followed the biomedical model and strongly advocated drug treatment as a first resort met with his approval. The Rockefeller empire included drug industries. It may not be entirely a coincidence that Flexner, a white upper-class man, found no merit in six of the only eight institutions which permitted black students at that time, nor in *any* of the ones which admitted women.

The 'alternative' institutions were not only not given funds, but forced to close. The Rockefeller and Carnegie Foundations were politically powerful, and legislation outlawing the practice of healing by anyone except graduates of the approved schools was quickly enacted. Tough laws against homeopaths, midwives and chiropractic gave the white, middle- and upper-class male medical establishment a virtual monopoly on the vast industry of health care.

This monopoly is being challenged today, but its legacy is still strong. So-called alternative therapies may no longer be actually illegal, but they are not covered by basic health insurance either, nor are they likely to be in the near future. The medical profession is a very powerful lobby group, quick to protect its own financial interests. It has been slow to acknowledge the merits of approaches other than its own.

The medical approach

Until recent years, the characteristics of the medical approach could be summed up, in general terms, as follows. A doctor treated the symptoms of disease, using a specialised approach and generally intervening in the disease process with drugs or surgery. He or she was trained to value emotional neutrality and objectivity; it was considered a bad thing to 'become involved' with a patient. Pain and disease were regarded as negative states, to be alleviated by the doctor, if at all possible. The doctor was the expert and the patient was seen as dependent, without any active role to play in his or her own healing. Body and mind were separate entities, and treated as such. The only reliable guides as to what might be going on in a patient were quantifiable ones — tests, charts and so on. If a doctor couldn't diagnose the cause of a problem, it would be referred to another medical specialist. The processes of pregnancy and birth, though not exactly falling into the category of illness, definitely required the supervision, or even the medical intervention, of a doctor.

Since the doctor's income was directly related to the number of consultations which can be squeezed into the hours available, and many people seeking medical help do so for symptoms which have no clear-cut organic cause, it's not surprising that all too often the consultation ended up being a relatively superficial affair. In more than two-thirds of cases a drug, which may or may not have been of some benefit to the patient, was prescribed.

Perhaps because most medical schools teach little or nothing about basic nutrition, many doctors have tended until recently to scorn the whole subject and heap ridicule on any practitioner who suggests that the things we eat might have something to do with our general health. The practice of chiropractic, homeopathy, acupuncture and all the other traditional medical systems has until now been dismissed as quackery, in spite of their long and careful development and their proven effectiveness in aiding the healing process in many instances.

The notion that illness may not always be an enemy, but a signal that a person needs to make the life changes which are a natural part of our growth as human beings, has been heresy. So has the idea that, in many cases, the best treatment is no treatment at all; what is really needed is a chance to rest and allow the body to heal itself.

The medicine practiced by the majority of doctors today is known as allopathic medicine, which means the treatment of disease and its symptoms. It focuses very little on prevention, or on health. In both Australia and America, approximately 97 per cent of the staggeringly large (and relentlessly increasing) health care budget is spent on treatment, with the tiny remainder of 3 per cent going into preventative and educational areas.

None of the above criticisms would matter much if the dazzling growth in medical knowledge and expert technology had resulted in better general health for the population. It hasn't. That's the problem.

As David Phillips states in his book *New Dimensions in Health*, the world's store of scientific knowledge doubled in the decade of the 1960s. So did the world's crime rate, its number of hospital admissions, and its spending on public health. Health care is now the third largest industry in the US, and the same is true of Australia.

In spite of the virtual eradication of many of the diseases which killed our own grandparents; in spite of the huge increases in public spending (more than US$50 *billion* in the US in 1979) on medical care; in spite of the medicalisation of almost every phase of human life, there has been no increase in life expectancy in the last quarter of a century, nor any reduction in the number of people who are ill.

The conquered diseases have been replaced by new ones. The incidence of chronic states of anxiety, allergy, depression and fatigue is growing at an alarming rate. More and more people suffer — and die — from degenerative diseases. Childhood cancers, once almost unknown, are becoming terrifyingly commonplace. The incidence of asthma is skyrocketing. The mortality rate for major cancers hasn't changed significantly in the past thirty years in spite of new drugs, more sophisticated radiation and surgery techniques, and public education about early detection.

The 'medicalisation' of modern life

Iatrogenic or doctor-induced illness, usually as a result of surgical complications or prescribing drugs wrongly, is estimated to account for as many as 20 per cent of all hospital admissions (up to one million annually in the US). A British study of 350 randomly chosen coronary patients who were in similar stages of illness found that the death rate for those who were being treated in intensive-care units in hospital was significantly higher than for those who were convalescing at home. And from Israel comes the interesting story that when doctors went on strike for a month in 1973, the death rate in the country dropped by 50 per cent (from Ross Horne's book *Improving on Pritikin — You Can do Better*).

Our general health is deteriorating while we are surrounded by an abundance of food, more leisure, increased education and all the other factors which, it was once assumed, would lead to greater general well-being. Dr John Harrison, in his book *Love Your Disease: It's Keeping You Healthy*, points out that the majority of Australians take daily medication of some sort, approximately half of which has been prescribed by a doctor and half not. Anything taken into the body changes its chemistry; any substance powerful enough to have an effect is capable of harm as well as benefit. When you consider how many of us also use nicotine, alcohol and caffeine on a regular basis, a picture emerges of a population almost universally under the influence of drugs. Is this really a healthy situation?

In his book *Medical Nemesis*, Ivan Illich argues that the increasing 'medicalisation' of modern life not only produces clinical iatrogenic illness, but obscures the actual social conditions which are making us unhealthy, as well as eroding our belief in our ability to heal ourselves. 'Modern medicine has become a major threat to health and its potential for social, even physical, disruption is rivalled only by the perils inherent in the industrialized production of food.'

This questioning of our belief in medical solutions is echoed by the distinguished immunologist, Sir Macfarlane Burnet. 'The real problem of today is to find some means of diminishing the incidence of diseases of civilisation. Nothing from the laboratories seems to have any relevance to such matters.'

Even the infectious diseases, which the medical model seemed so effective in controlling, are not a thing of the past. Indiscriminate use of antibiotics has encouraged the growth of increasingly drug-resistant strains of bacteria. Widespread and rapid international travel has made the transmission of these, as well as virulent influenza and AIDS, virtually uncontrollable.

The new picture of illness in our society shows that the largest area consists of chronic states such as circulatory disorders, obesity, arthritis, alcoholism and other addictions, and psychiatric illness.

Although some of the symptoms of these illnesses can be alleviated, they cannot be 'cured'.

The second large group of disorders are upper respiratory tract infections, allergies, stress-related conditions such as recurrent tension headaches, anxiety states and ulcers. These are usually treated by medication, either prescribed by a doctor or self-prescribed.

The medical or surgical conditions in which technical intervention is of benefit — and the ones to which the majority of medical education and public health spending is devoted — is the smallest group of all. Medicine, at the interface of humanity and technology, is still putting its energy for the most part into the technology, while the incidence of illness which cannot be treated in this way is increasing all the time.

Dr David Collison, an Australian physician, states flatly that of the patients seen by doctors in general practice who don't come in with a broken bone, a virus or some similarly straightforward condition, up to 80 per cent cannot be given any sort of worthwhile assistance. According to him, approximately half of all our visits to doctors are for symptoms which are neither diagnosed nor treated properly. Something is clearly wrong.

Science's traditional views are changing rapidly now in the fields of physics and biology. Current medical practice, too, is feeling the effects of new ways of thinking about disease.

Holistic Medicine

Dr Nicholas Bassal, an originator of the Australian Wholistic Practitioners' Network, says that there is tremendous and increasing interest in holistic medicine among doctors today. The network, which was formed in 1984, has been deluged with health professionals applying for membership and information, and many of the applicants are medical doctors who want to learn more about alternative healing methods.

'Wholistic medicine is a system of medical care which emphasises personal responsibility and fosters a co-operative relationship with all those involved, leading toward optimal well-being of body, mind, emotions or spirit,' Dr Bassal said in an interview about the establishment of the Wholistic Practitioner Network. 'A wholistic practitioner regards illness as a lack of balance in the whole person, rather than a breakdown of one of the parts of the body.'

This new movement among doctors is encouraging. But it's also not good enough to simply blame the more traditional members of the profession for a situation which we have all helped to create. Our health is our own responsibility, and it's up to us to become informed about it. We must stop expecting the medical profession to produce magical solutions for complex problems. We must take more interest in how the tax dollars which go to health are spent, and make our opinions known to the people who spend them.

What we need now is a return to the common sense which has always maintained that the whole is greater than the sum of its parts. We need the wisdom to know that, when it comes to dealing with a living being, there is an essential life force which can never be perceived by a reductionist method. It is this force which makes the organism function smoothly, and illness results when it is out of balance.

Luckily, there are many people who have always had this wisdom.

5 *Holistic Health Therapies*

'The well-being of man is influenced by all environmental factors...that quality of air, water, and food...and the general living habits.'

Hippocrates

The holistic or natural view of health is, of course, not new. The word itself, derived from the Greek *holos*, meaning whole, was coined quite recently. The concept, however, is as old as human knowledge and one of its main cornerstones.

It was Jan Smuts, the first Prime Minister of South Africa and a biologist by training, who introduced the word. In a work published in 1926 and quoted in Richard Grossman's *The Other Medicines*, Smuts argued that 'the creation of wholes...and of wholeness generally as characteristic of existence, is an inherent characteristic of the Universe. And holism is the inner driving force behind that progress.'

Holistic health therapies share the fundamental belief that a human being is an integrated living system. Further, we are integral parts of the larger systems, such as the physical and social environments, with which we interact. We are dynamic, indivisible beings and everything in our inner and outer environment is interrelated.

By looking at ourselves in this way, it's possible to drop many negative and counterproductive beliefs about disease. The idea that we are innocent victims

of a world swarming with hostile microbes is an
excellent one to dispense with, for a start. So is the
idea that there is nothing we can do except hope that
chemical drugs (the good guys) will prove stronger
than the germs (the bad guys). As Lewis Thomas, one
of America's most distinguished biologists and medical researchers, says in *The Lives of a Cell,*

> Watching television, you'd think we lived at bay, in
> total jeopardy, surrounded on all sides by human-
> seeking germs, shielded against infection and death
> only by a chemical technology that enables us to
> keep killing them off. We are instructed to spray
> disinfectants everywhere…We apply potent anti-
> biotics to minor scratches and seal them with plas-
> tic…We live in a world where the microbes are
> always trying to get at us, to tear us cell from cell,
> and we only stay alive and whole through diligence
> and fear…
>
> The man who catches a meningococcus is in con-
> siderably less danger for his life, even without
> chemotherapy, than meningococci with the bad luck
> to catch a man.

The incidence of life-threatening bacterial diseases
has certainly been reduced by the discovery and use
of antibiotics, and even more by modern plumbing
and water treatment. But we can never come to terms
with today's life-threatening diseases by continuing
to see them as variants of the older bacterial ones,
for they are not.

Today we need to turn our attention to environmental factors, and to our own innate healing abilities. Then perhaps we can start to use our common
sense and our considerable powers to deal with the
very real threats to our well-being posed by the dirty

air, dirty water and contaminated foods of contemporary industrialised society.

This is not a new approach, but a return to a well-established reservoir of human experience and wisdom. Many of today's most effective therapies have much in common with traditional practices.

Traditional medicine

Healing techniques used by tribal shamans often focused on bringing a person's unconscious conflicts into the open, where they could be understood and dealt with. Shamans used dream analysis, group discussion, hypnosis, guided imagery and psychoactive drugs to help their patients. Illness was usually seen as the result of environmental influences, unconscious blocks or problems in social relationships. Ever-increasing numbers of therapists operate from exactly the same premises today.

What is traditional medicine? The Americans call it 'alternative medicine'; the British call it 'natural medicine'. Whatever it's called, it has been with us for thousands of years and even now, while Western scientific medicine is at its height, it's still the primary form of medical care used by most of the world's people.

The World Health Organisation as quoted in *The Other Medicines* has defined traditional medicine as 'the knowledge and practices used in diagnosis, prevention and elimination of physical, mental or social imbalance, and relying exclusively on *practical experience and observation* handed down from generation to generation, whether verbally or in writing'.[12]

Traditional or folk medicine is not a single body of knowledge or practice, of course, stemming as it

does from the varied experiences of people living
in different conditions and with different beliefs. But
just as allopathic medicine can be generally characterised by its focus on separate biological or physiological processes and its treatment of symptoms
rather than causes of disease, so traditional or natural
medicine has tended toward a view that in order to
deal effectively with any illness, it must be seen in
context. Whatever the actual techniques used by a
traditional healer — herbal remedies, acupuncture,
psychological or spiritual rituals, modification of diet
or reduction of food intake — the emphasis is on
restoring the lost balance of the individual so that
the innate tendency toward health can operate
properly.

Herbal remedies

One of the oldest strands of traditional healing comes
from the knowledge that some plants have powerful
medicinal properties. The study and practice of herbalism extends back for millenia. A burial site in Iraq,
for instance, some 60 000 years old, contained the
pollens of the same therapeutic plants which are still
used today by the herbalists of that area. Similar
evidence from Peru, Mexico, North America,
Babylonia, Egypt, India, China and Greece shows a
well-developed awareness of the healing properties
of local plants. The Assyrians and Sumerians may
have been the first to put such knowledge into writing. The temple of Karnak, in Egypt, was decorated
with carvings of useful medicinal herbs brought from
Syria around 1500 BC by an expedition sent for the
purpose by King Thutmosis II. Ancient Chinese and
Indian texts, and the Bible, make extensive references

to the use of plants for a variety of ills.

The Australian Aborigines prepared and used herbal remedies for all manner of physical problems. After two centuries of dismissing this knowledge as unimportant, non-Aboriginal Australians are today beginning to understand the enormous usefulness of substances like the healing, antiseptic ti-tree oil. The Aborigines had a wide range of inhalants, antiseptics and linaments. They were expert in medicinal botany and possessed knowledge of literally thousands of remedies which they applied in the treatment of wounds, infected sores, headache, gynaecological matters, colds and other respiratory disorders. Some of the substances they used, like the alkaloids reserpine and atropine, have become extremely potent additions to the Western pharmacopoeia.

By the Middle Ages, European and Celtic knowledge of herbal remedies was extensive. Unfortunately, the very effectiveness of folk healers led to their persecution by the Church. Christianity had abandoned the healing role exemplified by its founder, Jesus, by about the twelfth century, and it opposed the efforts of lay people to apply their traditional knowledge to help the sick. The ascribing of healing powers to witchcraft, and the cruelty of the methods used to suppress the people versed in folk medicine, is one of the darker passages of 'civilised' history. A great deal of useful information went underground, and a great deal has been lost.

It was, in fact, a big step backward when the medieval Church chose to realign disease and healing with the forces of evil. Much earlier, Hippocrates had carefully dissociated the treatment of illness from the influence of superstition and the supernatural. He had taught that disease was a natural phenomenon and established a system of diagnosis and prognosis based on rational observation.

Hippocrates believed that the role of the physician was simply to assist the natural healing force which is present in all living beings. The word 'therapy' comes from the Greek 'to attend'; the therapist was seen as an attendant or assistant to the process of healing. The Hippocratic doctrine emphasised that health is a state of balance, that environmental influences play a large role in health and disease, that mind and body are interdependent and that the most important thing for a physician to remember was to **do no harm.**

The 5000-year-old Chinese system of medicine shares the same basic orientation. Illness is not regarded as some intruding agent, but a natural symptom of change in the inner balance of a human being. It is not the general classification of diseases which matters so much as the individual diagnosis. Since the same symptoms in different people may stem from different causes, they should not necessarily be treated the same way. Instead of treating symptoms, traditional Chinese healers try to counteract the individual cause of imbalance, reasoning that if the underlying cause can be corrected, the symptoms will disappear. In this process, the subjective knowledge of both healer and patient are of utmost importance.

The validity of the intuitive factor in diagnosis and the awareness that any given drug or treatment has different results on different people is, of course, acknowledged by many modern medical practitioners.

Too often, however, it is relegated to secondary importance and patients are treated as though they are interchangeable units rather than unique individuals.

Fasting as a means of cleansing

Chinese medicine uses herbalism, massage, acupuncture, breathing exercises, corrective diet and fasting as therapies. Many of these were also used by the practitioners of the Ancient Mysteries, a group of spiritual teachers who travelled through Egypt, India, Greece, Persia, Scandinavia and the Celtic world many centuries ago. They prescribed periodic fasting as a means of cleansing the system and prolonging life.

These ideas were adopted by the Celtic druids, who included fasting as part of their religious training, and recommended five days of total abstinence from solid food in cases of illness.

Two thousand years ago, the Essenes of Judea prescribed fasting for health, longevity and clear thinking. They influenced an Egyptian sect called the Therapeutae whose fasts on natural raw juices, lasting from one day to one month, formed the basis of the 'miracle healings' for which they were famous.

In other parts of the world, fasting as a means of strengthening the healing power within has been understood for a long time. The practice is common among Pacific Islanders and in the Middle East, where many people cleanse themselves periodically either by totally abstaining from food, or taking only fruit juice. Both Buddhists and Hindus — a huge percentage of the world's population — recognise the spiritual and physical benefits of fasting and do it on a regular basis.

The wisdom of traditional remedies is still acknowledged in most parts of the world. Even in Western Societies most of us have favourite remedies for common ailments that stem from empirical knowledge passed down from generation to generation in our families.

The limitations of modern medicine

When it comes to their own health, doctors often still apply the older precepts too. In a fascinating essay on modern medical practice, Lewis Thomas describes the result of an informal survey he carried out into the habits of the people responsible for designing our present health care system — the 'well-trained, experienced, middle-aged, married-with-family internists'. He found that these medical specialists almost universally refrain from doing the very things they recommend for the rest of us. Few of them have routine medical checkups, for instance, and they almost never allow themselves to be X-rayed, except for dental work. Thomas found, further, that these architects of our public health policies quite strenuously resist surgery, laboratory tests and the use of antibiotics and most other drugs. And not just for themselves; they discourage the use of such things by their families too.

As Thomas explains in *The Lives of a Cell* the evidence of the 'do as I say, not as I do' syndrome of doctors is simple:

> The great secret, known to internists...but still hidden from the general public, is that most things get better by themselves. Most things, in fact, are better by morning.

The medical profession's public denunciation of the common sense many of its members privately make use of, however, has resulted in a widespread dismissal of natural therapies as occult and dangerous, inferior at best and outright quackery at worst. This is changing rapidly as the limitations of institutionalised medicine in dealing with new patterns of illness become more and more apparent, and as more and more people are demanding a holistic approach in treatment. But there have been dissenting voices among the doctors themselves for a long time.

In his *Treatise on Fevers*, published in 1666, the physician Thomas Sydenham observed wryly that many poor people owed their lives to the fact that they couldn't afford medical treatment. He urged practitioners to distinguish symptoms from diseases, arguing that, since a headache or a fever could stem from a variety of underlying causes, it was only logical that the proper treatment would differ too.

Oliver Wendell Holmes, Professor of Anatomy at Harvard, wrote in 1860 that

> I firmly believe that if the whole materia medica, as now used, could be sunk to the bottom of the sea, it would be all the better for mankind — and all the worse for the fishes.

The natural health movement

Advocates of cleansing to restore good health have sometimes been prevented from practising in the West, but they have never completely disappeared. Both Hippocrates and Paracelsus, a sixteenth century Swiss physician, considered abstaining from solid food to be extremely beneficial during critical periods of illness. These ideas persisted and strongly influenced the European natural health movement of the last century, especially in Austria, Germany, Switzerland and Scandinavia.

In Europe, it had long been the practice of wealthy people to take a 'health cure' at a fashionable spa, where simple diet, the use of natural mineral waters and hydrotherapy treatments proved effective in alleviating many chronic disorders. The other benefits — general weight loss, improved appearance and increased vitality — were appreciated too. The 'nature cures' of Priessnitz in the early nineteenth century, and the simple water therapies of Father Kneipp and the English Dr Gully, were a logical outgrowth of the popular spa treatments.

In more recent times, two well-established institutions, the Bircher-Benner clinic in Zurich and Otto Buchinger's Bad Pyrmont Centre have supervised thousands of therapeutic fasts. The success of these centres in treating chronic illness, obesity, addiction and emotional problems with a simple regime of eating lightly, taking raw foods, reasonable exercise, fresh air and sunlight made a strong impression on the growing natural health movements in both America and Australia.

The principles of vegetarianism were widely popularised in America by Bernard Macfadden, the founder of naturopathy, and in Europe by Dr Rudolph Steiner. The clear and comprehensive information about the value of a proper diet in the books written by Herbet M. Shelton, founder of the Americal Natural Hygiene Society, has helped many people in more recent times.

TOXIC BUILD UP

6   *What on Earth are We Doing?*

'A society based on cash and self-interest is not a society at all, but a state of war.'

William Morris

It would take an armful of books the length of this one to present all the evidence of the injurious effects of the millions of tonnes of chemical poisons which are sprayed, dumped, buried and burned in our planet's soil, air and water every year. Such books exist, and they make alarming reading. More information on the impact of our short-sighted use of dangerous substances is being published all the time. It all carries the same message.

Once again, commonsense should have given us that message from the start. Poisons used to 'control' insects, animals and plants — to kill living organisms — harm people too.

In the last forty years, the synthesis of new chemical compounds has proceeded at a staggering rate. As Dr David R. Collison points out in his book on clinical ecology, *Why Do I Feel So Awful?*, a new compound is created and added to the environment at the rate of about one a minute in the US alone. The American Chemical Society has more than three million chemicals on its registry, almost none of which were in existence at the end of World War II.

We are adaptive creatures, but in our history until now we have only been required to adapt to small changes, and over a long period of time. The introduction of a huge range of unknown substances (even if they are not all such potent killers as dioxin and agent orange) into the environment is not something to which we can, or should, adapt.

Technological progress and hazardous substances

The widespread pollution of our air, water and food is not just an unfortunate incidental by product of technological progress. Our economic system is based on increasing profits and both production and consumption must continuously increase for this to be possible. The industrialised nations produce a bewildering array of products, some of limited use-fulness and dubious merit, which are heavily promoted to the consumer. The manufacture of drugs, synthetic fibres and plastics uses complex chemical processes which create millions of tonnes of chemical waste each year, all of it alien to natural life forms.

In the decade from 1970 to 1980, the amount of hazardous waste produced by American industry increased from ten million tonnes to thirty-five million tonnes. It costs money to treat such waste, and even more to recycle it. Manufacturers don't treat or recycle any more of it than they have to, and have frequently managed to influence governments to relax even the safeguards which *do* exist in law.

When you examine the evidence of the irresponsibility, evasion and downright greed practised by many polluting companies, it becomes depressingly obvious that, as Ralph J. Gleason said 'in the naked pursuit of profits, a good American company will do anything'.

The only real answer for ourselves and for the ecosystem of the planet in the long run is to cut back on the production of harzardous substances. In the short term, however, we can take steps to protect ourselves individually. Both approaches require a radical change in our attitudes as producers and consumers.

Only a few years ago, the majority of people probably still thought that 'they' must know what 'they' were doing. We were led to believe that 'they' — the manufacturers, the farmers, the pharmaceutical companies, the government agencies which set standards and controls — wouldn't allow harmful things to be done to us.

But recently there was the case of Love Canal in New York State. The ironically named Love Canal was a site where toxic chemical wastes had been dumped for years, gradually leaching into the soil and water of the surrounding area. The rate of birth defects, liver and kidney disease and cancer among people living nearby grew too high to be ignored. When investigations were carried out, the whole locality was declared a disaster area and the inhabitants evacuated.

The US Environmental Protection Agency estimated in 1979 that there were at least 50000 similar dumping sites in the US, and that the wastes in less than 7 per cent of them were 'properly disposed of'.

There was the massive disaster at Bhopal, in India. There was the evidence of the effects of agent orange on the men exposed to it in Vietnam, and their children. There was Chernobyl.

The recent grounding of the *Braer* off the Shetland Islands, with its disastrous spill of nearly 100 million litres of oil, was only the latest in an ever-lengthening list of such environmental catastrophes. There was the *Torrey Canyon* which spilled 875 000 barrels into the English Channel in 1967, the *Urquiola* spill off La Coruña, Spain, in 1976 (80 million litres); the massive 254 million litres spilled near the French Coast in 1978 by the *Amoco Cadiz*; there was the *Exxon Valdez* off Alaska, the *Aegean Sea*, again near La Coruña; the *Maersk Navigator* spill in the Straits of Malacca, only days after the breakup of the *Braer*.

We're told that such accidents are inevitable; it's the price we (and all the marine species) have to pay for our huge dependence on oil. But surely, accidents which can be foreseen are *not* inevitable. We must put pressure on our governments to enforce strict controls on the sea transportation of oil. If it must be shipped by sea, then it must be shipped in seaworthy vessels, double-hulled and in good repair. At present, nearly three-quarters of the world's large crude oil carriers are more than 15 years old and due for replacement. Many are in disrepair, and many fly flags of convenience from nations whose shipping inspectors may be overworked and undertrained. The tankers sometimes take risky short cuts to save time and money. The *Braer* was taking such a short cut; it should never have been where it was when it was struck by the storm in the North Sea.

Oil spills aren't the only problem that exists in

this region. Each year, more than 50 000 tonnes of
heavy metals are dumped into the North Sea alone.
The Rhine and Elbe rivers have carried a heavy load
of pollutants since the beginning of the Industrial
Revolution, and for the past 50 years, ever-increasing
loads of toxic chemicals in addition.

There are indications of serious collapse of the
marine life chain in the area. Widespread coastal
algal blooms are one sure sign of trouble, while
the death of nearly 20 000 harbour seals in
1988-1989 from a viral disease is believed by
many biologists to have resulted from a collapse
of the animals' immunity, due to overexposure to
chemical and heavy metal contamination of their
environment.

The 1986 fire at the giant Sandoz chemical
factory near Basel, in which more than 30 tonnes
of pesticides, fungicides and dyes were released
into the Rhine, literally killed the river for 200
kilometres. It's difficult to comprehend the enorm-
ity of such a crime against nature. The officials
monitoring the effects of the spill found that company after company was discharging amounts of
chemicals into the Rhine which far exceeded the
permitted limits.

Acid rain and nuclear waste

In the spring after the spill from the *Exxon Valdez*,
when the great migration of millions of Canada
geese, ducks and other water fowl made their way
north, as they have for millenia, to their Arctic
nesting grounds, they didn't find the sparkling
water and rugged rocks which had always met

them before. Instead there was a chemical waste-land, dead and black with slippery, stinking fatal oil. The Americans set up gas-fired cannons to try to discourage the flocks from landing, but without much success. Instinct is very strong in birds. They don't understand about modern technology. They cannot adapt suddenly to a lifeless, poisoned environment. Neither can we.

Oil-based processes are dirty, and coal-fired indus-tries are even worse. When coal is burned, large amounts of nitrogen oxide and sulphur dioxide are released into the air. When these gases combine with water vapour and oxygen in the air, sulphuric and nitric acid are produced. These acids are washed down in rain as acid rain, killing great stretches of forest and polluting lakes so that the web of beautifully balanced life which has develop-ed over hundreds of thousands of years is wiped out in a generation. The forests and lakes of eastern North America and Northern Europe are dying; some are dead. The life force of a forest or lake is both strong and fragile. It cannot survive such relentless attacks.

More and more, we are beginning to see our own relationship to the rest of the world. We are not separate from the earth. It is a living entity, a unified system, and we are its creatures. Our life depends on the health of the planet. And wherever we dump our poisons, it's still our own back yard.

This is a particularly sobering thought when it comes to the disposal of nuclear waste. Plutonium, which can cause cancer in the invisible dose of one-millionth of a gram, remains active and dangerous for 500 000 years. At present, even without the

nuclear by-products of military research, the waste
from 'peaceful' nuclear processes will amount to
some 690 million litres of radioactive rubbish by
the year 2000. This material must be isolated
from all living things. Since we have no idea how
to store such waste safely for even a century, let
alone 5000 centuries, we're leaving our descendants
a very treacherous legacy indeed.

The way our food is grown and treated

Another alarming aspect of the modern chemical
era is the whole field of food production. Again,
in the last forty years, the way that our food is
grown and last treated has undergone a revolution.
Throughout human history, farmers grew a variety
of crops and practised sound conservation principles. They rotated crops and enriched the soil
with organic waste like animal dung and vegetable
matter. Soil is not inert. It's a living substance,
filled with dynamic material and thousands of
micro-organisms which interact to provide the
basis of life itself. It was a system of sunlight,
water, and natural chemicals processes. It worked.
It worked so well that our species thrived.

But 'progress' dictated that it should work better.
The growing synthetic chemical industry found, in
farming, a rich area for expansion. Its tests showed
that production could be spectacularly increased
by abandoning traditional methods and putting
large areas of land under cultivation of a single
profitable crop, adding artificial supplements and
fertilisers, and controlling weeds and pests by
spraying the crop with specific poisons.

The spectacular increase in production, however, didn't last long. After only a few years of these practices, the organic content of the soil was so reduced that more and more fertilisers were needed, while pests adapted to the poisons and became resistant to them. Without humus to hold the moisture, the soil became dry and hard, so more powerful machines were needed to till it. The dry soil is more subject to erosion by wind and water. And as the ecological imbalance caused by overuse of chemical fertilisers, herbicides and insecticides led to an increase in crop diseases, more and stronger poisons were needed.

It's a classic vicious circle. Since the end of the Second World War, farmers have used six times as many chemical fertilisers, and twelve times as much insecticide, on their land. In spite of this, crop losses from invading insects have doubled in that period.

The methods used in raising animals and poultry, supposedly the source of the high-quality proteins we've been told we need to be healthy, have also suffered from the 'better living through chemistry' mentality. Cows, sheep, pigs and chickens are routinely dosed with large amounts of antibiotics to reduce the diseases which are rife in modern farm factory-lots and battery pens, as well as sex hormones to promote unnaturally fast rates of growth. These potent drugs collect in the animals' fats and tissues. When we eat meat, they're passed along to us.

Approximately 60 per cent of the cost of our food today is the cost of the energy used to produce it, mainly petroleum and its by-products. The basis of our food is no longer soil, but oil.

The widespread use of chemical fertilisers, pesticides and herbicides has resulted in large amounts of toxic chemicals seeping into the underlying water table, to resurface far from the original site of use. Since most pesticides are mixed with petroleum distillates which have been shown to be good at destroying the body's natural immune system (and are carcinogenic in themselves) this is bad news. As Rachel Carson said nearly thirty years ago in *Silent Spring*, 'As crude a weapon as the cave man's club, the chemical barrage has been leveled against the fabric of life.'

Like the holistic movement presently growing among doctors, however, there is a swing of the pendulum back to sanity among some of today's farmers. 'Sustainable agriculture' — growing food by traditional methods which don't deplete the soil or poison the environment — is gaining ground. Organic farming is increasing and will continue to do so if we're willing to support it by seeking out the products grown this way. In Australia, the National Association for Sustainable Agriculture has set up a national certification scheme for organic farms, and the number of successful applicants is growing all the time.

But the bad news doesn't end with the way the majority of food is grown, however. What happens to it between farm and supermarket is even more outrageous.

To increase profits, manufacturers have to make their products cheaper. More and more, the foods we buy are not only storehouses of the chemicals used by farmers in their growth, but they are loaded with synthetic colours, flavours, stabilisers, emulsifiers and texturisers from the arsenal of more than 12 000 additives presently allowed. Few of these have undergone much testing for safety. Even fresh fruit and vegetables are dyed, gassed and waxed to improve their colour and retard spoilage.

Refined foods and additives

In addition, many foods are 'processed'; refined, in the case of flour and sugar, or chemically broken down and then reconstituted. The simple rules of a good diet — that foods should be **natural**, consisting of organic food elements in an unaltered state, and **whole**, neither refined nor enriched, and **free of poisons**, without toxic chemical residues or any other additives — are getting harder and harder to follow.

Probably the single worst aspect of our Western diet is its heavy reliance on refined sugar and flour. Flour keeps much better without its wheatgerm and bran because weevils can't live in it as well. It's not nourishing enough. After being hulled, refined, sterilised and bleached the wheat has lost much of its protein and other nutrients, and nearly 90 per cent of its fibre. All that's left is starch and chemicals. It's not just nutritionally poor, but actually bad for you. White flour contains ten times as much cadmium, for instance, as wholemeal flour.

And refined sugar — which the average Australian now consumes at the rate of fifty kilos per person every year — is even worse. It contains no nourishment at all, just empty calories, and it leaches calcium and magnesium supplies from the body as it's digested. Between them, these two refined

carbohydrates are responsible for much of the
unhealthiness of the average Western diet.

Many processed foods are heavily laced with
both sugar and salt, as well as with a range of
chemical additives to change or preserve the food's
appearance and texture. Increasingly, the processed
food is not just frozen, dried or canned in order
to destroy dangerous bacteria, but padded out
with cheap 'replacer' ingredients. At the moment
the researchers are trying to find ways to use
substances like ground-up chicken feathers as
such replacers.

It's not easy to keep up with all the many forms
of food adulteration being practised today. Standards for testing the safety of the additives are
minimal, and in Australia the food labelling laws
are such that not all potentially dangerous substances have to be acknowledged. Collison, whose
book contains an excellent detailed summary of
present knowledge about all aspects of food
processing and adulteration, quotes the director
of the British Industrial Biological Research
Association as saying 'food additive toxicology is
not a science which seeks to understand the biological effects of chemicals on humans, but merely
a technology designed to produce animal test data
sufficient to gain permission from governments
for the use of the additives'.

Even this minimal standard is not always met.
Much of the American research on the safety of
food additives is carried out by commercial laboratories, some of the largest of which have been found
to falsify their data in order to allow manufacturers
to put the product into use faster. In deciding which

additives are to be allowed here, Australia relies
heavily on such overseas data.

The real testing of these substances is being
done on **us**, the consumer. And we have, in fact,
discovered through experience that some of the
commonest dyes cause hyperactivity in children,
and that many additives provoke allergic reactions.
In Australia today each of us eats about two kilos
of chemical additives per year, and that's a very
conservative estimate. In Britain the figure is
between three and seven kilos annually, which is
probably more accurate.

We simply **do not know** what we're eating a lot
of the time. It's a case of (as Miles Davis said) 'I'll
play it first and tell you what it is later'. Which is
OK for jazz but not for what we eat and drink.
Since we don't know the long-term effect of eating
these substances, nor what happens when they're
all combined together in our bodies, it would seem
to make sense to avoid them as much as possible.

This means avoiding most of what's sold as food
today. In general terms it makes good sense to
stick mainly to fresh fruit and vegetables, properly
cleaned and prepared, and bread made from
wholegrain flour. A book called *The Additive Code
Breaker* is available which can help you identify the
substances which are currently added to common
foods. These are simple devices which can be
installed to remove most of the cumulative toxins,
such as sodium fluoride, from your drinking water.
They'll be described in detail later.

These are things everyone needs to consider,
because everyone today has some level of toxic
residue from environmental sources. Without

taking measures to counteract it, the level will simply keep increasing.

An American researcher, Dr H. Rudolph Alsleben, did an exhaustive study over five years to determine exactly what people had in their bodies. More than half a million tests on people of all ages and backgrounds were carried out. Dr Alsleben found four kinds of tissue destruction in every single person studied: heavy metal poisoning (lead, arsenic, mercury, nickel, cadmium and strontium); arteriosclerosis; infection and malnutrition. In everyone.

7   *The Inner Environment*

'The armour we wear — the armour of technology separating us from the rest of the world — has created us lately in the condition of exiles. Nature exists within us as well as without, and we are become, therefore, exiled from ourselves.'

John N. Bleibtreu

The growing chemical contamination of our outer environment has an equally serious inner equivalent. For many reasons, some of which we've looked at in terms of the dominance of allopathic medical theories in this century (and particularly the startling success of certain drugs in dealing with bacterial illness) we have become increasingly prone to 'taking something' for everything which ails us. In fact, we take drugs even when nothing particular is wrong.

Studies of drug use show that, in addition to the widespread consumption of prescribed drugs, a very large number of people are regular users of over-the-counter medications. Encouraged by advertisers to think that we're looking after ourselves by doing so, we seem to be in the habit of taking 'a little something' whether we're ill or not.

Other studies have estimated that the rate of increase in the use of legal pharmaceutical drugs is around 25 per cent per year. Certainly, medication is sometimes necessary, even life-saving. But since there is no such thing as a drug without side-effects, the rapid increase in drug consumption generally is an alarming trend. Even the most 'harmless' substances often extract a high price from chronic users.

Aspirin, for instance. Generally thought to be harmless, aspirin in various combinations (usually with codeine, caffeine and/or phenacetin) was found to be taken in large amounts, especially by women. In some areas it was common for up to one-third of the population to be taking several doses daily. Almost every household had its bottle of aspirin in the bathroom, and possibly in the kitchen, bedroom and motor vehicle as well.

When it was discovered that the people who were taking all this aspirin had a very high rate of gastric ulcers and serious kidney disease, phenacetin was replaced in the compounds with paracetamol. Once more the drug was promoted as 'safe', and heavily advertised for indiscriminative general use. Recent evidence suggests, however, that it is no safer than the older compounds. And people continue to take it daily, 'just in case'. In case of what?

The general perception that medicine is, by definition, a good thing, is a strong factor working against public health. This is complicated by the fact that many ailments cure themselves relatively quickly; if a drug is taken and the symptoms disappear (just as promised in the magazine or television advertisement) the drug is given the credit. In fact, the same thing would very likely have happened, perhaps even more quickly, without the medication.

At present, doctors recommend drugs of one sort or another in two-thirds of all their consultations with patients. An average of nine prescriptions per person per year is issued in the UK. This figure, high as it is, masks the much higher rate of drug-taking by the elderly. In that same year, the average number of prescriptions written for pensioners was twenty-two. And many doctors are saying now that much of this medication is unnecessary or even harmful.

The two most commonly prescribed families of drugs are the antibiotics and sedative hypnotics (tranquillisers and sleeping pills). Although the antibiotics are one of the most specifically success-ful drugs in treating bacterial illness, their overuse had led to many strains of bacteria now being resistant to them. They are sometimes prescribed for viral illnesses like flu, on which they can have no effect, and many people are also getting sub-stantial 'accidental' doses in the meat they eat.

The second group of drugs is often prescribed to deal with a range of symptoms which really require changes in lifestyle — learning how to relax, how to handle stress, and how to make better decisions which lead to peace of mind. The sedative hypnotics are not harmless: 'minor' tranquilliser addiction is now a major problem, especially among women. They are even more dangerous when taken in combination with alcohol, which they often are. Dependence on these drugs occurs if they are used for any length of time, and withdrawal from them is a dangerous and difficult process. In spite of these well-known problems, vast amounts of minor tranquillisers and sleeping pills continue to be pre-scribed, which seems an indication of something seriously wrong.

It's easy to be critical of doctors for relying too

heavily on their prescription pads. But it's certainly not all their fault. Many doctors try to dissuade over-use of drugs, and some have developed very effective non-drug treatments for conditions like high blood pressure. There are some enlightened doctors who help many people by teaching them medication techniques and other stress-reducing alternatives to drug treatments. The problem is often that people demand some sort of medication, and will take their business elsewhere if the doctor doesn't 'give them something'.

The pharmaceutical industry

The pharmaceutical companies also bear a large amount of responsibility for the situation. It's in their financial interest to have drugs prescribed as a first resort, and they know it very well. That's their business. It's a big business, too. The annual turn-over of just four UK drug firms (Glaxo, Wellcome, ICI and Beecham) in 1986 was more than £70 million, not including over-the-counter medicines.

The drug companies spend an enormous amount of money promoting their drugs, both to doctors and to the general public. Nearly one-fifth of their sales revenue is spent on advertising, and much of this takes the form of gifts to individual doctors. Over the years this approach has proved highly successful.

Heavy propaganda about the 'miracle of modern drugs' is fed to the public in press releases and popular articles, so even doctors who have healthy scepticism about the process find themselves under pressure to go along with it.

In spite of the amount spent by the pharma-ceutical companies, however, not much infor-

mation about how the drugs work, or their contra-
indications and side effects, is actually presented
either to the doctors or to the rest of us. This is a
real problem, since no busy medical practitioner
could possibly keep up with the flood of new
research data produced each year. Their knowledge comes very largely from what the pharmaceutical companies tell them, and perhaps the
best that can be said about this selective information is that it actively promotes the use of drugs
as the main method of treating any disease.

The pharmaceutical companies have specifically
and successfully lobbied successive governments to
allow them to provide *less* information, claiming
that many ingredients shouldn't be listed because
they are trade secrets. So effective has this lobbying
been that many of these substances are not only
not disclosed on the labels, but they are not even
included in the prescribing literature, which is
the doctor's main source of product information.
Some people are highly allergic to the substances
used, but even their doctor can't tell whether
their reaction is to the drug itself, or to one of the
mysterious additives which have been permitted
to be kept confidential.

Efforts have been made over the years by concerned people to have more complete information
made available to doctors and consumers alike,
but it's been an uphill battle in many places.

The vested interests are powerful ones, and many
governments are reluctant to get tough with the
pharmaceutical companies, who pay taxes and
provide jobs, and who can always move their
manufacturing operations to more 'co-operative'

nations if requirements grow too stringent.

Except for antibiotics, which are toxic to bacteria in a highly selective fashion, most drugs, at best, treat symptoms without effecting the course of the underlying disease. In some acute cases, of course, drugs can save lives. But they can sometimes do real harm by suppressing pain which should not be ignored, for example, or by interfering with the body's ability to heal itself through fever and elimination, as in the case of a cold. The mood-altering drugs which are prescribed in such enormous numbers encourage drug dependency and do nothing about the life situation which has led to the sleeplessness, anxiety or depression.

Masking symptoms of distress is no solution. But should we blame doctors, who are after all not trained to deal with complex human problems, for their inability to help us cope with the social situations which are causing such symptoms?

The famous medical researcher Sir Macfarlane Burnet is certainly not the only doctor to question the prevailing overuse of drug therapy, but he's one of the clearest.

> When in doubt don't do it!
> When one uses non-biological substances from aspirin and barbiturates onward as drugs...one must be worried. Treatment of this artificial character may sometimes be unavoidable but, to use an old medical cliché, the over-all results are usually not encouraging.[20]

In addition to the problems of ineffective drugs and drugs with serious side effects, there is the additional factor that many people take drugs in amounts and in ways other than the way they are prescribed. Many people have their prescriptions filled and then don't take the drugs; others may take the drug in ways other than prescribed. Some researchers have estimated that up to 15 per cent of medical hospital patients have adverse reactions to their drugs, and that as many as 5 per cent of acute admissions are a result of such reactions. Certainly, at the very least, we need to become much more responsible in our use of drugs, and weigh the possible risks of any drug therapy against its benefits. This is all the more necessary because far too little is known about the effects of the drugs in use. Clinical trials are not perfect: a drug may well pass basic toxicology tests and still prove harmful for some people. In other cases, the drug is simply ineffective pharmacologically, although the strong placebo effect (your belief in its usefulness makes it work for you) may hide the fact.

In recent years, consumers' rights groups have published clear information on all aspects of legal drugs — how they work, what to beware of, and how to make informed choices about using them. Such directories often include lists and descriptions of the commonly prescribed drugs, and information about possible interactions of each substance with other drugs and even common foods. Such material is a valuable, even necessary, resource for individuals who want to take responsibility for their own health and well-being.

Clinical ecology

Aware of the limitations of conventional drug therapy, and influenced by the principles of holistic health, an increasing number of open-minded doctors are looking beyond the advertising of the drug companies for a way to help their patients. One of the most promising approaches is that of the relatively new field which is generally known as *clinical ecology*, whose practitioners argue very persuasively that a large number of people are suffering from symptoms caused by reactions to the foods we eat, and to the chemicals in our environment.

Clinical ecologists have observed that probably half the people who consult doctors get no help at all. What other profession, they ask, would accept a 50 per cent failure rate?

In their view, the great majority of contemporary health problems are unnatural in that they simply don't occur among people who still live as our ancestors did. They are caused by new substances in our environment, or by our diet. Both have altered far more rapidly than has our ability to adapt to them.

The practice of clinical ecology considers the whole person, and that person's relationship with their whole environment — its plastics, nylon, foods, gases and drugs. Treatment consists of identifying the substances which are making you sick, and eliminating them as far as possible.

The essential simplicity of this approach is radical, and so far many doctors have shown little interest in applying it. But support for it is growing, because it has proven effective in many thousands of actual cases over a period of some fifty years. People with a wide range of disorders that have not responded to conventional treatments get well, and stay well, when they avoid certain suspect substances.

One of the reasons why some doctors may be slow to accept this approach is because their training doesn't emphasise our biochemical uniqueness. Different people react to the same substance in highly individual ways. A food or chemical which is making one person miserable may have no effect on others in the immediate environment. Also, there may not be a clear association between the symptoms and the offending substance. Allergy has been described as 'the great masquerader' and can manifest itself in a bewildering variety of forms. It may require sophisticated detective work to find the culprit. The commonest symptoms of an allergy — a rash, nausea or fever, may not be present. Often the reaction develops gradually, over a long time, so it's hard to pinpoint.

In his book *Why Do I Feel So Awful?* Dr Collison describes the body's amazing and complex immune response. It's usually very efficient in producing antibodies to protect us against harmful antigens like bacteria, viruses and poisons. Sometimes, however, the immune system reacts against naturally occurring proteins and auto-immune disease develops, or it malfunctions, as in AIDS, so that diseases simply bypass its normal defences.

An allergy is an immune response to a basically non-threatening substance, like grass pollen. It's a mistake. The body perceives a danger when none is there. This is the process which occurs when you develop intolerance to a food, too. Protein in food is broken down, by digestive enzymes, through several stages. The final products are amino acids, which can be absorbed by the body. It appears that the protein in many foods, if unable to be digested, may pass into the bloodstream and reach organs and tissues where it is recognised as foreign material by the immune system, and attacked. The reaction to this attack manifests as allergic symptoms.

The ability of the immune system to respond appropriately can be damaged by many things, including infection, emotional stress, sudden weight loss, an accident, drug therapy or even changes in the weather.

One of the key theories of clinical ecology is that regular exposure to any food or other substance may lead to intolerance. It may take years, but eventually some molecules of the material, instead of passing through the digestive process, make their way into the bloodstream and provoke the immune response. Once this happens, every repeated exposure will inevitably trigger the negative reaction.

The person almost always adapts to the situation, and after a period when there are some symptoms of distress, they disappear. The person usually begins to crave the actual substance, because allergies are very closely allied to addiction. In satisfying the craving, whether it's for chocolate, bread, coffee or whatever, the damage continues to be done. The addiction cycles vary according to how long the substance remains in the body, from hours to days. In the final stages of the process, the adaption ceases to work and the person experiences constant symptoms of withdrawal and exhaustion.

The commonest symptoms of allergy or ecological illness are headache, persistent fatigue, muscle pains, arthritis and joint pains, high blood pressure, mood swings, depression, obesity and alcoholism.

These are the symptoms which bring many people to the doctor. They're the same ones which so often fail to respond to conventional treatment, and for which painkillers and tranquillisers are so often prescribed.

The food or chemical intolerance occurs as a result of individual susceptibility, combined with either one heavy exposure to the substance, or repeated smaller exposures. Constant exposure to any one material greatly increases the chance that intolerance may develop. This is borne out by the fact that the most commonly eaten foods are responsible for a majority of food allergies: coffee, eggs, milk and wheat.

To discover what may be causing the problem, a few days on a limited food programme, followed by reintroduction of suspected foods (the challenge test) is a very effective method. Since fasting reverses the process of accumulation of toxic wastes in the body, it strengthens the immune system at the same time.

In the case of our response to any of the 400 synthetic chemicals which have been recently identified in human tissue — one result of the 45 kilograms of chemicals presently manufactured annually for each man, woman and child on the planet — it is similar to that of food intolerance. There is usually an initial period of uncomfortable symptoms, then a variable time when the reaction goes underground. Finally, the ability of the immune system to cope breaks down, the masking effect disappears and any repeated exposure causes immediate and often very serious reactions.

The actual chemical allergens are in the molecules which are constantly being emitted from the things around us. Plastics, polyesters, polyvinyls, silicones, epoxy resins and fluorocarbons emit or 'outgas' at a high rate all the time, but even wood and stone release some molecules into the atmosphere.

Even more active, of course, are the specific poisons we spray under our houses, the pesticides we are encouraged to use frequently to rid our surroundings of even the most harmless insects, and volatile substances in cosmetics and cleansers.

The 'paranoid few' were right

As Dr Mark Donohoe said recently in a talk given to the Natural Health Society, there is a growing movement among doctors back toward a broader understanding of health. This is partly because the incidence of diseases like AIDS and chronic fatigue syndrome, both of which are characterised by suppression of the immune system, and neither of which respond to conventional treatments. 'The "paranoid few", who all the time believed that fluoride, chlorine, pesticides, herbicides and many others of the 47 000 registered chemicals are not good for us, were absolutely right,' Dr Donohoe said.

He sent blood samples from a number of his patients (suffering from chronic fatigue syndrome) to a specialised laboratory in America, to ascertain which toxic chemicals were in their bloodstreams. The results were dramatic. For chemical after chemical, the Australian blood levels were higher than for Americans — sometimes as much as ten times higher. Whole groups of chemicals were present in large accumulations — the chlorinated chemicals, the aromatic chemicals, the pesticides and herbicides. And, as one might expect, the older the people, the greater was the concentration of these toxins.

In his view, people are getting sick because they are *unaware* of the chemicals stored in their bodies, and therefore unaware of the need for detoxification. Until this century, our senses warned us about dangerous substances. But now, as Dr Donohoe says, 'we have a hazard from chemicals which science has made tasteless, colourless, odourless and toxic in incredibly tiny amounts. We don't realise the damage that we've done.'

We are victims of the 'boiling frog' principle, or pseudoadaptation. If a frog is put into hot water it will do everything it can to escape. It knows it can't survive such an extreme environment. But if it's put into cold water that's heated slowly, it doesn't struggle. It adapts bit by bit — until it's dead. Similarly, we adapt to the chemical contamination of our environment little by little, as the toxic residue in our tissues increases. For us, like the frog, the point arrives when we are overcome.

Some people appear to be much more sensitive than others to the substances in common use in our surroundings. These are the people now manifesting the symptoms of chronic fatigue, which include an overwhelming sense of tiredness and debility for no apparent reason. They are like an 'early warning system' which, if recognised, could lead the rest of us to question the idea that it's all right to spend our lives in a chemical smog. Those of us who are still well can make the changes which are necessary if we want to stay that way.

These chemicals cause immune suppression, thus allowing other diseases to establish themselves. Dr Donohoe, along with others, believes from his experience that **chemicals not normally found in the** body are unsafe in any dosage. There is no safe level. In spite of this, we are exposed to them constantly — every time we sit in a car, or on a plastic chair, or in a painted room. The amounts may be tiny, but the exposure to them is constant.

DETOXIFYING

8　*A Hospital is no Place for a Sick Person*

'Less is more.'

Mies Van Der Rohe

For a person who needs a surgical procedure or who is acutely ill, the expertise and technical support which is available only in a large, expensively equipped hospital staffed with expert nurses, anaesthetists, radiographers, physiotherapists and doctors is a wonderful and often life-saving resource.

Most of us, however, are seldom in such an extreme situation. More and more our problems are chronic or intermittent ones — allergies, fatigue, stress-related conditions and degenerative or lifestyle diseases such as hypertension, arthritis, depression and obesity. Hospitals are not the answer here. Such conditions require a change in the way we live. We need help with the immediate problem, certainly; but more than that, we need to learn how to make the changes which will not only get rid of the symptoms, but also strengthen our immune system and increase our general vitality so we can prevent their recurrence.

Whether our condition requires the expertise of a hospital or not, however, the optimal healing environment is one of peace and security. We need to have confidence in our surroundings and in the people who are working with us. We need a clean, calm, quiet place and the best of wholesome food (or none at all). We need to understand as fully as possible what is happening to us, and how, once we leave the hospital or natural health centre, we can stay well.

Without being unfair, I think it's true to say that the modern hospital, dazzling though its technical resources may be, seldom provides these things. It may be the best and indeed the only place to treat acute or disastrous episodes of illness and accident, but it's the worst possible environment for a convalescent.

Hospitals are often located on main urban thoroughfares, subject to the constant noise of trucks and cars and their foul emissions. Inside, they may be almost as busy. There is a constant internal traffic of staff and visitors. The last thing a sick person needs is to be exposed to frequent loudspeaker messages implying a state of emergency, unfamiliar odours, questionable food and the alarming awareness of sick and injured strangers all around.

Worried about the initial condition which brought him or her there, surrounded by an army of strangers and intimidated by the general atmosphere, the hospitalised person is likely to become passive, taking the proffered medication, submitting to the tests, ranging from the mildly embarrassing to the distinctly frightening, and hoping the doctor knows best.

An American doctor, Robert S. Mendelsohn, compared the hospital to a war. 'You should try your best to stay out of it,' he said. 'And if you get into it you should take along as many allies as possible and get out as soon as you can.'

But the only ally hospitals generally allow you to bring in with you is your faithful inner healer, and even this constant companion may be a little overwhelmed by the surroundings. It will be taken for granted that your presence more or less implies consent to eat the food provided, take the pills prescribed (even if you don't want or need them, such as sleeping pills) and generally cooperate with a minimum of fuss.

An alternative to hospital

There are alternatives to hospital. The number of healing and therapy centres based on principles of natural health has increased in recent years. Practitioners capable of supervising a treatment plan which includes the profound inner cleansing of a water or juice programme can usually be located by consulting local natural heath societies, naturopaths, homoeopaths and chiropractors.

At centres which base their therapies on natural health principles, you will find an atmosphere which is markedly different from that of hospitals. It will be as calm and quiet as possible, with no rush, bustle or sense of crisis. No drugs will be given, although people already on medication may need to continue taking it during their stay. There will be no invasive procedures. The food will be free of sugar, refined flour and chemical additives and the diet based largely on fresh fruit and vegetables.

At such centres, the emphasis will be on your own power to heal yourself. You will not be seen as a patient, nor encouraged to have a passive attitude toward your own health. Natural health therapists see themselves as allies of *your* inner healer, and will try to provide the best possible circumstances for your healing to take place.

Together with the practitioners in a natural therapy centre, you will discuss and decide on the programme to be followed in your particular case, although the therapists will be able to make suggestions based on their experience with similar cases.

You may be encouraged to take only water for a number of days, while resting as completely as possible. You may follow a regime of fresh juices. Or the choice may be a simple, healing rest, while eating a normal diet of whole natural foods.

If a water programme is undertaken, the staff will monitor it very closely. They will tell you what you may expect to happen at different stages, and will advise you on the best way of beginning and ending the programme. They will keep a careful eye on your progress and how you feel. Above all, a natural therapist will always act in a manner which acknowledges and respects the wisdom of your own inner healing power.

An important part of the role of any such therapist is that of teacher. This may be the single biggest difference between the experience of being in hospital and that of being a guest at a natural health centre. In addition to the individual consultations, there will generally be a rich programme of lectures and demonstrations which provide information and offer opportunities to have any questions answered. It's a process not just of temporary help but of permanent empowerment. As the well-known saying goes, if you give a hungry man a fish, you feed him for a day. But if you teach him how to fish, you feed him for life.

All the practitioners at centres which include

inner cleansing as a part of their therapy programme not only understand theoretically how
the process works; each of them will have applied
it in his or her own life. They won't be recommend-
ing that you do something they themselves have only
read about in books. They will be guiding you
through a process which they believe to be effective
because they've experienced its results in their own
lives. This is traditional wisdom at its clearest,
being passed on in a practical and ethical manner.

Inner cleansing: in breaking addictions

Although fasting is contraindicated for diabetes,
some cancers and a few other individual cases,
there is a very wide range of conditions in which
it can be of enormous use as a therapy. Near the
top of the list is substance addiction, which is
increasingly widespread in our society. When an
individual chooses freedom from addiction, there's
a lot of cleaning-out to be done — physically,
mentally and emotionally. Whether the addiction
has been to tobacco, alcohol, prescribed tablets
(sleeping pills and/or tranquillisers) heroin, cocaine
or any combination of the above, body and spirit
both need help during the transition to a drug-
free life.

A supervised programme at a natural therapy
centre is an excellent way to begin the process of
recovery from addiction. For one thing, it's a very
self-loving and self-affirming thing to do, as well
as a clear statement of intent to change. The supervised fasting or following of a natural diet helps
the body regain its normal balance as quickly as
possible, while massage, hydrotherapy and other

treatments can relieve some of the physical discomfort of withdrawal. Although long-term recovery from addiction may require sustained follow-up in the form of support groups, the first few days of abstinence and detoxification are crucial, and the therapeutic environment is an invaluable help.

Some people fear gaining a lot of excess weight when they stop smoking, and in this case the learning of new eating habits at such a centre can ensure this doesn't occur. The nervous system is severely stressed both by addiction and by the sudden withdrawal of the addictive substance, so the profound rest which is made possible at a natural therapy centre is extremely beneficial during this difficult period.

To change long-standing habits is one of the hardest things a person can do. Use of the substance usually results both in short-term pleasure and an avoidance of pain or discomfort, so there is constant reinforcement to continue the addiction. Conflict between the urge to continue and the urge to stop can result in severe anxiety and depression, which makes it even harder to make positive choices. Learning to practise relaxation techniques and other methods of dealing with stress in the safety of a supervised therapy programme is essential. The tension associated with actual physical withdrawal can be lessened through exercise, meditation, relaxation and breathing exercises and cognitive techniques; after the crisis of the withdrawal period is over, the techniques can continue to help the individual's recovery over the longer term.

This is important, because most people who are motivated to free themselves from addiction find the physical withdrawal tolerable. It's often not as bad as they feared, especially if a cleansing programme is followed during the transition. It's going back to their 'normal' life, but minus the crutch of their accustomed addiction, that proves overwhelming for most. It's a sad fact that approximately 2/3 of smokers, alcoholics and drug addicts have a relapse to the old patterns within three months, and in the great majority of cases these relapses were triggered by some form of emotional stress. Therefore it is of the greatest importance that effective methods of dealing with stress be learned at the beginning of recovery, and practised regularly. It's easier to take new ideas and habits on board in the context of an all-inclusive therapeutic experience, and such an experience is most likely to be found at centres based on natural therapy principles.

A treatment for osteoarthritis

As an example of how specific conditions are treated at such a centre, take Julia, who was suffering from osteoarthritis. The pain in her knees, hands and hips had progressed to the point where it seriously interfered with her ability to work, both in her job as a teacher and at home. Although her husband was understanding, the pain in her joints made sex difficult and this was causing emotional problems she had never experienced before. She felt old and unattractive. To make things worse, she had to give up gardening, which she loved, and the bush walks which had always been the high points of her family's excursions. The arthritis was robbing her of much of the joy of life. And it was getting steadily, inexorably worse.

Julia's doctor was treating her condition with a common anti-inflammatory drug used in such cases, called Voltaren. He had told her that, while it would relieve her symptoms to some extent, it could not improve the underlying condition. Probably that would continue to deteriorate.

All drugs have a number of side effects. In the case of Voltaren, they include gastrointestinal problems, nausea, heartburn, diarrhoea and flatulence. It can also cause headaches, tiredness, dizziness, ringing in the ears, insomnia and irritability. Asthma sufferers are adversely affected by it, and it can lead in some cases to peptic ulcers and kidney or liver disorders.

Although Julia was 'lucky' and didn't develop any of the more severe reactions, she did experience headaches, insomnia and irritability. Combined with her inability to do the things she liked and the fact that the arthritis itself was getting steadily more like a daily jailor, she gave up her job and withdrew from her friends and family. In time, all these negative life changes led to a serious depression.

Her worried husband accompanied her to the doctor, who prescribed Tryptanol, a trycyclic anti-depressant which combines alleviation of the symptoms of depression with sedative effect, so that Julia would sleep better. No-one knows how the potent tricyclics actually work, but they are effective in many cases, in elevating the moods of severely depressed people. Their side effects include an extremely dry mouth, blurred vision, confusion and marked, sometimes dangerous effects on the whole cardiovascular system.

Again, Julia was 'lucky'. She tolerated the side effects and as her depression lifted she began to adapt herself as best she could to a life which was increasingly restricted by her arthritis. Her doctor spoke to her about the possibility, at a later date, of an artificial hip.

Without a job and unable to take any part in many of her former activities, Julia began to read a good deal. One result of her browsing was exposure to information about alternative methods of treating the pain of arthritis. Feeling that she had nothing to lose, she had a series of treatments with an acpuncturist. These relieved her pain and even restored some movement in her knees and hips.

More important, the acpuncturist asked her about her diet. It was the first time anyone had asked Julia what she ate, although her doctor had recommended that she lose weight in order to reduce the burden of her joints. When the therapist discovered Julia ate an average diet — high in animal proteins, fats, starches, plenty of salt and sugar and all washed down with cups of coffee and tea — she told Julia to cheer up. With a thorough cleansing, followed by a change in diet, there was every reason to hope for substantial improvement in her condition. The acpuncturist recommended that Julia go to a natural health centre and she agreed.

When she arrived at the health centre, Julia discussed her condition thoroughly with one of the health practitioners. She was not really convinced that something as simple as abstaining from solid food for a few days could result in any long-term benefits for her, but she thought that she might at least lose some weight.

The practitioner recommended that Julia spend a day or two on raw whole foods, another day on juice, and then a few days on water only. During the course of the cleansing programme, her intake of Voltaren would be gradually reduced. She would have hydrotherapy treatment every day, with alternate cold and hot packs applied to the painful areas. And she was to rest.

In the quiet surroundings, Julia courageously followed this regime to the letter. As her medication was cut down and the cleansing process followed its natural course, the pain in her joints was sometimes very severe. She stuck to her guns, however, aided by the information that what was happening was the normal inflammatory process, which had been suppressed by the anti-inflammatory agent, Voltaren, doing its work to repair the affected tissues around her joints.

By the time she had completed an eight-day fast, she was free of both her medication and a good deal of the pain. Years of accumulated toxins had left her system, along with more than seven kilos of excess weight. She spent a further few days on fresh diluted juices before resuming eating, consuming only natural foods.

During her stay, Julia attended many of the lectures and by the time she was ready to leave, she understood more about the underlying causes of arthritis, as well as how the body is capable of regulating and healing itself. She knew which forms and combinations of foods were acid-forming, and aggravated the symptoms. She had learned what would be an optimal diet for her, and how to prepare the foods which would form the basis of her new method of eating. She had lost a further four kilos of weight and was relatively pain-free without having to take drugs. Best of all, from her point of view, was the fact that management of her previously crippling arthritis was not only possible, but in her own hands. She knew that to do about it. She knew what worked and why.

Two years after leaving the centre, Julia is still following the diet which made such a difference for her. Occasionally she feels she needs to spend a day drinking only juices, but her arthritis is a thing of the past. She has resumed teaching, works in her garden and makes love with her husband, all without any recurrence of arthritic pain.

The benefits of prevention

Not all conditions respond so quickly or completely to the cleansing programme. It is not a miracle cure. But it is of enormous benefit in many, many cases which have not responded to allopathic medical treatment. And its preventative aspect cannot be overemphasised. The increased vitality and sense of wellbeing which follows a programme of inner cleansing is reason enough to give yourself the experience.

And it's more necessary today then ever. None of us can entirely avoid the chemicals, pesticides and toxic wastes in our environment. We are the first generation of human beings to live in such conditions and although we've been told that none of these things will hurt us — that all the substances are tested and strictly controlled — current scientific evidence supports the commonsense knowledge that continual exposure to harmful substances over a long period of time has a cumulative effect. How can we poison our surroundings without poisoning ourselves? We can't.

9 *Fighting Back*

*'Nothing is contrary to the laws of nature, only to
what we understand about the laws of nature.'*

St Thomas Aquinas

Toxaemia has traditionally been defined as a
condition characterised by the presence of bacterial
toxins in the blood. Recently, however, the definition
has been widened to include the presence of any poisons or waste products such as residues of chemical
contaminants which affect the immune system, and
which the body tries to eliminate. There is convinc-
ing evidence that a diet which is too high in protein
can contribute to toxic buildup as well.

Toxaemia is the basis of many pathological
problems. Most disease syndromes have an underlying, related condition of toxaemia. It's important to
understand this fundamental fact in order to see why
adopting a detoxifying way of life is so vital for us now.

When the buildup of toxins in the blood becomes
too great for your system to handle, a condition known
as *enervation* results. This is an unpleasant and
happiness-destroying condition, marked as it is by
a lowering of vital energy. The functioning of the various eliminatory processes is impaired, the immune
system is weakened and you become more susceptible to both bacterial and viral diseases.

When enervation occurs, most often as a result of
stress or an overwhelming burden of toxicity, elimination becomes much less efficient and the amount
of poison stored in the body becomes progressively

greater. A clear account of how this happens is given by H.M. Shelton, one of the leading members of the American natural hygiene movement, in his book *Fasting For Renewal of Life.*

In the enervated state, all the body processes function below their optimum efficiency. There is poor digestion, and therefore faulty assimilation of nutrients. There is poor elimination, and therefore an increasing buildup of toxic levels in the blood. In time, this vicious circle leads to a crisis in the form of illness, in which the body makes a heroic effort to rid itself of some of the accumulated wastes.

If this process is suppressed by taking drugs to counteract the symptoms, not only is the natural healing action thwarted but an additional load of powerful synthetic substances is added to the overburdened system. In an enervated condition, drugs may simply add to the problem. What's really needed when the body signals that it's having trouble — whether its expression is in the form of a cold, deep fatigue, aches and pains or any of a number of other symptoms — is **rest**. The body has important work to do, and it needs your cooperation to do it. Not only do you have the right to rest when you need to, but you are the only person with the power to structure your life so that you can.

Supporting your inner healer

Your inner healer needs support to do its necessary rebalancing. If you rest, drink pure water, reduce your food intake or abstain from food altogether for a short time, a good deal more energy will be available for the vital process of detoxification.

The body cleanses itself continuously, and does

it most efficiently if the diet is high in fibre and contains enough fluids. Because of the current overload of both internal and external pollution, however, many people in industrialised societies are living with a level of toxicity which is close to crisis point. A relatively small amount of additional stress caused by overwork or personal problems, a period of poor nutrition or some other negative factor can lead to a situation where the body must get rid of the poisons faster than normal elimination procedures can operate. The mucous membranes of the mouth and nose may be pressed into service or the temperature raised; both these processes are effective in disposing of body waste.

The symptoms of these processes are, of course, exactly the ones people are exhorted to suppress by taking over-the-counter cold remedies and headache tablets. Often the advertising assures you that by popping the pills, you can continue to work as hard as ever. Of course you're too busy to be sick! Such advertising often relies on your response to an underlying moral message that it's your **duty** to keep on functioning as normal, even though you're ill. It's presented as a virtuous way to act. It shows you're responsible. To whom?

The implied corollary is that only wimps or people whose work is unimportant can afford the luxury of resting when their bodies need it. Another favourite device of the drug companies' advertising is to make parents feel guilty if their children are sick. No caring parent would allow their child to suffer when there's an available remedy, would they?

But such illness is the body's effort to restore its deeper health. As Yagyu Tajima No Kami expressed it in *Zen Swordsman*: 'Let yourself go with the disease, be with it, keep company with it; this is the way to get rid of it.'

This may seem like a radical idea to people who believe that it's stoical to keep on operating at full capacity no matter what signs of distress their bodies exhibit, or that it's foolish to suffer discomfort when relief is as close as the pharmacy. But the fact is that the body heals itself when given the chance to do so, and understanding this can make a big difference in how we react to the messages from within.

The problem with constant suppression of the natural detoxification process is that the buildup continues and the manifestation of illness will inevitably become more serious as time goes by. How sick do you have to be before you allow yourself to rest? How incapacitated? Many people carry on as normally as possible until hospitalisation and surgery are deemed necessary.

You don't have to. By understanding and cooperating with yourself, you can prevent the development of graver, chronic problems. Suppressing a fever or taking antihistamines for a cold are really acts of sabotage against yourself.

When toxaemia is present, the bloodstream needs to be cleansed. This is made possible by rest. Taking only water permits this rest, as does spending a short while on a natural juice diet, or a cleansing diet of fresh fruit and vegetables. These are powerful aids to the body's efficiency in doing what it needs to do to restore its balance. The more you work **with** the process and not **against** it, the more you will benefit in both the short and the long term.

This simple concept of resting when your body

shows a need for it is up against stiff opposition in contemporary society. So often our self-worth is tied to constant activity and to operating at maximum capacity, making it extremely difficult, psychologically, to let go even for a little while. We feel it's self-indulgent in the worst way to put our real needs first.

We need to give ourselves permission to be healthy. If this requires some sort of moral justification, then consider the eventual cost, both to yourself and to society, of allowing chronic illness to develop when it can be avoided by a little enlightened self-interest in the form of a sensible response to indications that detoxification is required.

The importance of rest

The anabolic or building-up processes of the body — cleansing and cell regeneration — increase during periods of rest, relaxation and sleep. And rest is greatly aided by reducing the amount of food you eat. For most sedentary workers, digestion is the single greatest user of the body's energy reserves. When this energy is made available for other things, the body's ability to eliminate toxins and wastes is enormously enhanced. Not only does the digestive system get a break, but the load on the circulatory, respiratory, glandular and nervous systems is also considerably reduced. At the same time, the excretory function not only continues but increases. The cleansing benefits that take place when you rest the body depend on this fact.

A period of real rest lets an overworked, overstressed body perform the vital cleansing of which it is usually incapable. No healing can occur in a body stretched to capacity and requiring all its energy to carry out ordinary functions. And modern eating habits burden the body with almost continual digestion.

When the system is overloaded and particularly when your diet is poor, your food itself may not be properly digested. If you continue to force food into your system at such times, there's a further strain on your internal resources.

When your body indicates that a period of detoxification is needed, even a short rest can do a lot of good. You don't have to wait for symptoms of distress. Regular reduction of the amount of energy you expend can strengthen the immune system, cleanse the blood and increase your vitality. Subjected as we are to such an overwhelming array of chemicals and contaminated food, it makes sense to build up our defences while we're still functioning relatively well.

Food is not the enemy; on the contrary, eating an optimum diet is in itself a cleansing programme. There's a long tradition of using natural foods for healing and it works as well today as ever, if you make the effort to supply yourself with organically grown, chemical-free whole foods. The basic cleansing diet is not complicated. It consists of fruits, vegetables, whole grains and seeds, eaten uncooked as often as possible.

Such a diet is detoxifying in itself. It improves the efficiency with which your cells use oxygen. It aids your metabolism, so wastes are disposed of more efficiently. It also prevents further buildup of toxic garbage, since you're consuming fewer chemical additives and avoiding the refined foods which rob your system of minerals.

The whole question of what constitutes an ideal

diet is, of course, subject to enormous debate. There are literally hundreds of books on the subject and although most of them stress the dangers of the typical Western diet — high in salt, fats, refined flour and sugar — they seldom agree on much else.

Obesity and reducing diets

Complicating the issue is the epidemic of obesity in our society. According to some estimates, half of all men over twenty-five, and a third of women, are significantly overweight. In the public mind the practice of 'dieting' is associated with self-denial, deprivation, difficulty and a host of confused motives. When attempts to diet are made these often lead to feelings of failure. Reducing diets simply don't work for most people. Any weight loss that takes place is often regained.

There's a good reason for this, and it's directly connected with poor nutrition and toxaemia. Weight loss actually depends less on the number of kilojoules consumed than on the efficiency of the metabolic process. The metabolic rate is the rate at which kilojoules are burnt in the presence of oxygen within the cells.

Muscle tissue is very active metabolically, while fat cells are not. The body creates some fat cells specifically to store excessive toxins, more or less out of harm's way, when the toxic level is too high for it to deal with through normal elimination. These fat cells often take the form of cellulite. Being sensible about its own ecology, the body tries to store its dangerous wastes where they will do the least harm. As the Danish doctor Kristine Nolti put it, 'Excess fat is nothing less than a poison depot in an over-acid organism'.

People who eat a toxic diet — and that's a good many people, increasingly including children — will tend to become fat not only because of the excessive kilojoules of a junk diet, but because the body will make more and more fat cells in order to store the garbage. Going on a series of low-kilojoule diets where weight is lost quickly and then regained is just about the most counterproductive thing an overweight person could do.

One reason for this is that the body may slow its metabolism even more during the course of the diet, conserving its energy in the face of what seems to be a threat. Another problem is that some of the weight lost is glycogen (a carbohydrate stored in the liver) or muscle. When weight is regained, these cells are often replaced by fat, so your fat-muscle ratio is altered in favour of fat, leading to a further decrease in your metabolic rate.

On the all-too-common Australian diet of refined foods, the waste from sugar, bleached flour and all the chemical additives is simply more than normal digestion can handle effectively. People get fat on this diet not only because it's so high in kilojoules, but because their bodies are doing their best to protect themselves from the problems caused by such foods. Only real nutrition — giving your body what it needs for health — can solve the problem. Following diets which are based on limited portions of nutritionally inadequate food is not the answer.

Another problem with crash diets is that quite unpleasant reactions can result from the sudden release of toxins into the blood as the fat cells are burnt. A slow, steady detoxification of the body is preferable. The too-quick method actually leads to rebound eating. The intense craving for food, especially sweet and fatty foods, is a biological reaction created by the organism's need to protect itself from the sudden overload of poisons. When too many acid wastes go into the bloodstream, the resulting trauma can lead many dieters into the syndrome of binge eating. This phenomenon plays havoc with the body's inner balance.

Since a body with a high level of toxins in its cells uses much of its available energy in trying to cope with wastes, one way or another, a common result of toxaemia is lack of vitality, sluggishness, chronic fatigue and depression. Another is obesity. Many people in our society are overfed but undernourished.

On a proper diet, the biochemistry of the body is rebalanced and both excess weight and excessive hunger disappear. When you're getting the nutrition you need, you feel satisfied. The body is neither greedy nor stupid. Food cravings and extra fat are symptoms of deprivation, not self-indulgence.

Chronic overeating may be a sign of food intolerance/addiction. Continuing to eat foods you're sensitive to leads to a very high level of toxic waste in your body. The only solution is to eat properly. Otherwise, your digestive and endocrine systems are under constant stress, and there will be deficiencies in the enzymes needed to break your food down into forms your body can use. A good diet gets rid of cravings by supplying real nutrients and normalising the digestive function.

Biogenic, bioactive, biostatic and biocidic foods

In her excellent book called *The Biogenic Diet*, British health writer Leslie Kenton describes four classes of foods in the following way.

The *biogenic* foods are those which are full of life energy. They are the ones which are actually capable of generating new life — nuts, sprouted grains, wholegrains and legumes. They are the best possible foods for regenerating cells and tissues, and providing high-quality sources of energy.

The foods she calls *bioactive* are good detoxifying agents. These foods — fresh fruit, vegetables and herbs — are still very much 'alive' and they are capable of stimulating metabolic processes and renewing cells.

The *biostatic* foods — wholegrain cereals, low-fat dairy products, free range eggs, cooked vegetables and legumes — provide productive bulk in a healthy diet and do little or no harm when eaten in reasonable quantities. The fibre in such foods strengthens the vital eliminative function of the body.

The final category is that of the *biocidic*, or life-destroying foods. Here we find white sugar, white flour, most meat and poultry, fatty dairy products, processed foods and all the favourite junk snacks such as crisps, candy and chemically flavoured foods and drinks. These foods increase the body's toxicity and interfere with proper metabolism.

A diet consisting mainly of biogenic and bioactive foods, supplemented by some biostatic ones, leads to regeneration of cells and hormones, helps restore the proper function of enzymes, gets rid of excess toxins, reduces overweight safely, and prevents the development of food allergies and binge eating.

The vitality of foods is an important factor, too. Fresh, raw whole foods provide far more of the essential nutrients than other foods. Enzymes are living things, and they're destroyed by cooking.

Such a diet is high in fibre and a good source of the purest water in the world — that contained within the cells of fresh fruit, vegetables, and sprouted seeds. This water contains electrolytes, vitamins, organic minerals, proteins, amino acids, natural sugars and other essential nutrients. Drying, baking, cooking and all forms of food processing get rid of this precious natural water.

Living foods help protect the body from accumulating toxic wastes in two ways. They contain less to begin with, and their active enzymes aid in the steady release of stored wastes from the tissues. The enzymes are organic catalysts which are required for proper digestion and utilisation of nutrients by the body. The entire metabolic process depends on them. There are many different enzymes needed by the body, each one carrying out a minutely specific role. A sufficient supply of all the necessary enzymes appears to be a crucial factor in maintaining immunity to many degenerative diseases.

The enzymes present in whole raw foods support your body's own enzyme production, because they are the exact ones needed for their own digestion. When the enzymes are destroyed by processing, your body has to make up the deficit from its own reserves. And the ability to do so is seriously impaired by a bad diet.

10 *Giving Yourself a Break*

'Now I see that the secret of making the best persons,
Is to grow in the open air and to eat and sleep with
the earth.'

Walt Whitman

So you're starting to suspect that our modern chemical environment may not be the ideal seedbed for long-term good health? Or that you could lift your game regarding the foods you've been eating? Perhaps you're simply open to the idea of giving the process of detoxification a chance to show you what it can do for you.

OK. How do you go about it?

As outlined in Chapter 2, abstaining from food greatly aids the body's ability to get rid of accumulated metabolic wastes. It's a perfectly natural process. Its benefits derive from the deep rest it allows the body. In order to get the most good from it, therefore, you need to be in an environment where you can let go of the ordinary activities and stresses of your daily life for a little while.

In the natural health centres of Europe, America and Australia, fasting is considered an invaluable prelude to a healthier lifestyle because it cleanses the bloodstream, increases vitality, sharpens the senses and strengthens all the natural body functions. It leaves you fit and ready to change.

Fasting at a natural health clinic

If the idea of using the power of fasting as a bridge between the way you've been living until now, and the way you'd really like to live, appeals to you, it's ideal to undertake it in a supportive situation such as a natural health clinic. You'll enjoy peaceful surroundings, have the rich resource of a variety of relevant information, and receive lots of encouragement in making your transition to a natural, non-toxic lifestyle. Last but not least, you'll have a good deal of freedom from the inevitable demands of your work, your relationships and your own programming to keep busy.

Adverse reactions

The staff at a natural health centre will have supervised thousands of fasts. They'll monitor your reactions and discuss them with you as you begin to throw off the accumulated toxins in your tissues and bloodstream.

Many people have some unpleasant effects because of the generally high level of toxins today. There may be headache, lethargy, diarrhoea or an upset stomach during the initial few days. The hands and feet may feel colder than usual. The tongue will probably exhibit some furriness and perspiration odour may change. These reactions occur because of the rapid elimination of poisons from the system, and generally pass quite quickly, within twenty-four to forty-eight hours. Hunger generally disappears in that time, too.

Because body and mind are essentially one, you might experience emotional effects. You may find that you feel more vulnerable than usual, for example, or a little sad. This can occur because you're not resorting to familiar ways of escaping your feelings, like having a quarrel with your partner or eating/drinking to cover them up. Letting go of any addictions, whether to nicotine, foods or relationships, can leave you feeling uncomfortably open and exposed for a while. This state can be very positive, showing the way for inner changes which will leave you stronger in the long run. Deprived of your usual props, you may find important realisations and understandings coming to the surface where you can deal with them clearly. Sometimes long-buried memories rise up in an atmosphere which allows you to pay attention to yourself.

In a similar way, drug users or people who have worked with toxic chemicals occasionally experience the disorienting sensation of tasting or smelling a substance they haven't taken or been around for years. This is a clear illustration of the fact that the body is using the opportunity to get rid of deeply stored poisons. All these things pass away in time. There's nothing wrong with feeling them; it's all part of the inner strengthening and cleaning.

If you suffer from a chronic disease, or are cutting out some medication or quitting smoking at the same time, supervision is necessary. The same is true if you plan to abstain from food for more than two or three days. Fasting is neither dangerous nor complicated, but there may be elements in the underlying condition of the faster which require knowledgeable observation.

There are some medical conditions which preclude fasting, so discuss it first with people experienced in the process. Diabetics on insulin should not fast, nor should people with some forms of cancer or renal problems. And if you're taking certain drugs, such as tranquillisers or medication for hypertension, you can't simply discontinue them. Obtain expert advice in such cases. And beyond respecting a child's lack of appetite when ill, a small person should never be put on such a regime. Finally, if you're afraid of the process, it's probably not a good idea. A positive state of mind as you begin is important if you're going to get the most out of it.

The great majority of people, however, can only benefit from the complete rest. Since your vitality and even your biological aging depends on the condition of your smallest vital links — the cells — the process of cell regeneration and rebuilding which cleansing stimulates will leave you feeling good and looking better. If you're overweight, you'll shed a welcome amount of fat. You certainly won't lose strength, because even in a prolonged fast the number of muscle cells doesn't decrease in number. They **do** decrease slightly in size, but are rapidly replenished when food is taken again.

At the end of the fast, your eyes and skin will be clearer, your blood pressure may be normalised, you will have increased energy and stamina, a clearer mind, better digestion and more flexible joints. You'll be ready to embark with enthusiasm on a more satisfying and natural way of life.

Under ordinary conditions, many of us find it difficult or impossible to allow ourselves a period of complete peace. Or we may want to, but our living situation doesn't permit it. Family obligations or the lingering, guilty feeling that we should be *doing something* may make it hard to rest completely at home.

Our usual surroundings may be noisy, especially during the day, and noise is just as polluting and stressful as toxic air or water to an organism which is working on healing itself.

The most valuable aspect of undergoing an initial cleansing at a natural health centre, of which Hopewood is a good example, is that everything is designed to encourage you to rest as much as possible. The surroundings are serene and harmonious; the activities which are available are gentle and relaxing ones; the foods and juices are as free from chemicals and additives as possible. You'll be supported in slowing down as much as you can and avoiding every type of emotional and physical stress.

Fasting at home

If you decide to experience a cleansing on your own, however, talk it over with a natural health practitioner before you begin. It's also sensible to have such a person to communicate with if anything arises which puzzles you during the process.

You're more likely to get a headache or other physical reactions if you've been eating foods to which you're sensitive or intolerant. A heavy coffee habit, for instance, can exact its revenge this way. But the response will pass fairly quickly, and it's a sure sign that some powerful work of cleansing is taking place.

It's often recommended that you prepare for a fast, especially if you've been eating a diet high in heavy or refined foods. Preparation consists of a few days' cutting down on such substances — refined sugar, meats, coffee, alcohol. Increase your intake of fresh and living foods in order to give yourself a head start to the detoxification process. A day or two on fresh fruit or vegetable juices completes the preparation for abstaining from solid foods.

It's important to drink uncontaminated water during your fast. Distilled water is available in bottles from health food stores and many supermarkets. During the fast, you should drink only when you're thirsty. You can't force the elimination process by drinking excessive amounts of water; you just increase the burden on your kidneys and although the expulsion of water will be greater, the expulsion of toxins won't be. Just pay attention to your body; if it wants a drink, it'll let you know.

And **rest**. Don't decide to combine your abstinence from food with a concentrated exercise program or by continuing on with most of your usual activities. There's just no point. Certainly, if the weather is pleasant, sit in the garden or doze a little in the shade. Enjoy a warm (not hot) bath once or twice a day. But you should **allow yourself to spend most of the time quietly in bed**. Shocking idea? Good idea! This is not only a chance to let your body become clean, but an opportunity for you to get in touch with your deeper self. Your centre.

Our society trains and educates us to perform a multitude of complicated functions. It places so little value on quietness and peace of mind, however, that when we are left entirely to our own devices, we are often at a loss. If you find you need diversions, choose them carefully.

If you enjoy a comic movie on the television or video, by all means watch it. But the violence and overwrought drama of many shows, and the apparently endless supply of bad news from the outer world, can get along without your passive participation for a few days. It'll still be there when you resume your ordinary activities. In the meantime, give yourself a break. Strengthened and renewed by a period of fasting, you'll have much more energy to *do* something about the things which concern you when you return to the fray.

Similarly, choose your reading material with some care. This is a time of nourishment for *you*, so use it to give yourself something truly worthwhile. You've stopped putting garbage into your body; give your mind and spirit the same consideration.

Tapes of beautiful music or material which nourishes your spirit can sink more deeply into a consciousness at rest. Journal writing, dreamwork, creative visualisation, deep relaxation and meditation are activities which don't drain your energy, but help in the regeneration process that's occurring at every level.

It goes without saying that any poisonous habits such as smoking or taking drugs will sabotage the benefits of a fast. And it's worth noting that for many people who want to quit smoking, it's not harder but *easier* to do in conjunction with a cleansing fast.

The length of the fast

How long should your fast be? To some extent, this depends on your state of toxicity at the beginning. It also depends on how long you can realistically devote to the process. If you have less than a week, it may be advisable *not* to undertake a water program. For periods of only a few days, it's often recommended that you spend a day or two on fruits and vegetables, three or four on pure juices, and then resume the fruit and vegetable diet to round it off. A significant amount of cleansing can take place on such a regime.

If you can clear a longer space in your life, then the introduction follows the same pattern. After a short period on whole foods and juice, you abstain entirely from foods, both liquid and solid, and take only water for several days. If you want to spend more than two or three days on a total fast, however, you should plan to do it under qualified supervision.

Proponents of natural health used to believe that major benefits only occurred when you followed the fast to its natural conclusion. That conclusion didn't happen so long as the body was still undergoing some measure of detoxification. The end of such a period is marked by a spontaneous return of natural hunger. In other words, the body itself signals when the fast should come to an end.

Since such a process may continue for weeks or even months, this is simply not an option for many of us. Contemporary natural health practitioners are of the opinion that even a limited physiological rest is of enormous value in the detoxification process. A good deal of inner cleansing and healing can take place in a short time, as long as it's followed by adopting a cleansing diet. Even as little as one or two days on fruit, or juices, can substantially increase your vitality and inner health. As Greg Mathieson of Hopewood says, 'even a week can regenerate people so that they go out sparkling'.

At this stage some part of your late-twentieth-century mind may be vigorously protesting: 'But I haven't got a week to spare! I barely have time to do everything as it is!'

How long did it take you to get the necessary skills to do your job? Twelve to twenty years at school, plus training courses and refreshers from time to time? How long did it take you to learn to drive a car? Two or three months? Four? Six? How long did it take you to learn to type? Use a computer? Play the guitar? The piano? Speak another language? Swim properly? How long did it take you to learn how to parent your children? Cook? How long did it take you to learn how to do any of the things you presently consider essential to your life? How much extra time did you manage to squeeze out of your busy schedule the last time you fell in love?

We're talking about feeling better *right now*, as well as creating the basis for ongoing good health *for the rest of your life*. We're talking about taking a *simple step to counteract the poisons* that are slowly but surely killing many people in our society. You are the only person who can decide on your own priorities. You're the boss.

Fasting ground rules

To sum up the basic ground rules for your first experience of conscious detoxification — your first fast — perhaps the first nearly complete rest you've ever had:

1 If you suffer from a chronic disease, are taking daily medication, or have the time and inclination to fast longer than two or three days, either go to a natural health centre or embark on the experience under the guidance of an experienced practitioner.

2 If you're going to fast at home, prepare your environment carefully so that you will be able to do as little as possible during the time you're abstaining from food. Explain what you're doing

to your near and dear and make sure you have their support. It's always a good idea to have contact wth someone experienced in the process whom you can contact if necessary.

3 Surround yourself with relaxing, uplifting materials to make use of if you get bored. And give yourself that vital permission to **let go of stress and unnecessary activity.**

4 If you've been eating a heavy diet, taper off for two or three days before you take solid food. Eat fruit and vegetables only for a day or two, then juices. During the fast, drink clean water only. At the end of the fast, reverse the process. Juice, then fruit and vegetables, followed a couple of days later by moderate amounts of grains and protein foods.

5 Take warm baths or showers while cleansing. Avoid extremes of all kinds. And keep yourself comfortably warm.

6 If you find yourself distressed for any reason, talk it over with someone who knows what's happening, or gently break the fast. It's not an endurance contest. Listen to your body. Trust yourself.

7 Remember that whether you're fasting primarily for the regenerative, detoxifying effects or for weight loss, the benefits will only be effective if you follow a cleansing diet after the fast.

8 Almost all health problems benefit from fasting because metabolic functions are improved in all tissues, cells and organs. Fasting gives the body a chance to clean and heal itself.

9 Keep your activities and exercise to a minimum, and keep them gentle. Don't roast yourself in the sun. Fresh air, deep breathing and plenty of total rest will increase the benefits of the fast.

11 *The Cleansing Diet*

I'm hungry! I'm hungry!
For good things to eat
For Sugar Jets, Sugar Jets
(Whole toasted wheat)

American billboard advertisement

To continue and build on the detoxifying benefits of
a fast, or to attain the same results more slowly over
a longer period of time, your basic diet should serve
you in two absolutely fundamental ways. It must
give you the nutrients you need to build healthy
cells and tissue, and it shouldn't be adding any
more toxins to your system. What it **contains** and
what it **doesn't contain** are equally important.

Fulfilling these two needs, which sounds simple,
requires conscious choices. We are literally surrounded by garbage masquerading as food. This state of
affairs is well documented in the works of many,
many qualified health writers, but the trend toward
a daily diet which is toxic at worst, and empty at
best, relentlessly continues. Why?

Our historical background is one factor. The
traditional diet of much of the Western world has
always consisted of the hearty, sustaining food
of northern Europe, from where a considerable
number of our ancestors originated. Living as
they did under conditions where fresh fruits and
vegetables were available for only a short time each
year, and foodstuffs had to be stored for the long
winter months, there was quite naturally a heavy

reliance on grains (which kept well) and meat, which could be preserved by salting and smoking. It may not have been an optimal diet but it provided sustained energy for people living in a cold climate. They also needed a heavier diet because they worked harder physically, in general, than people do today. Their grains were largely unrefined, and the meat, fish and poultry were completely uncontaminated by synthetic hormones, antibiotics, pesticides, herbicides and residues of heavy metal.

In what was often a marginal diet, fats, and especially dairy products, were an important energy source. Fresh meat and sweets were rare treats for all except a wealthy minority. Salt and spices were costly luxuries.

The ability to provide your family or guests with such expensive items as meat, wine and sugar was, until very recently, a sign of wealth and status. Important occasions like weddings, birthdays and religious festivals are still celebrated in the traditional way by conspicuous feasts of these foods.

Every day is a feast day

But now, surrounded by the affluent consumer society which we've developed since the industrial revolution, every day is a feast day. The sorts of foods which ouﬢ great-grandparents regarded as treats for special occasions — roast chicken, beef, wine, rich desserts — are ours whenever we want them. And if our programming to want them isn't strong enough, it's fortified by heavy advertising.

'Feed the man meat.' 'Sugar — a natural part of life.' 'Ginger ale tastes like love.' And so on. Ninety-nine per cent of all food advertising is for products

you don't need and shouldn't eat. Why is it that these
are the foods that are so incessantly promoted, especially to our children? Because they're the ones that
make the biggest profits for the food industry.

The plain truth is that the 'average' Western diet
could hardly be worse. It is directly as a result of
the 'average' diet that the 'average' Westerner will
die of heart disease or cancer (according to contemporary statistics, fully half of all Australians will die
from heart disease alone); the 'average' woman suffers
premenstrual syndrome to some extent and will develop osteoporosis later in life, and the 'average' person over twenty-five is obese.

Another reason why we eat too much of the foods
which have been shown conclusively to be bad for
us is because we learn, from babyhood, to see sweets
and other junk food as some sort of personal reward.
They make us feel as though someone loves us. We
'indulge' ourselves with them when we're overwhelmed by the frantic pace of our lives, or because
we feel alone. Binge eating, overweight and all forms
of addiction are part of the high price we exact from
ourselves when we feel powerless. We can't change
the world, we feel. But we can make ourselves feel
better for a little while by giving ourselves a treat.
We apply our childhood lessons. A treat is sweet, or
salty, or alcoholic; something that makes us feel pam-
pered for a few minutes. We try to ignore the long-
term effects.

We are encouraged by the food industry to believe
that our diet may be dangerously short of protein
(as no doubt our ancestors' sometimes was). We
literally 'eat like kings', taking in enourmous over
doses of salt, sugar, fats and refined foods. We often

compound the problem by consuming a huge meal relatively late in the day — a meal loaded with heavy, hard-to-digest animal fats and proteins, plenty of salt and sugar, and probably alcohol.

To make the situation worse, we're confounded and confused by the advice of various 'experts' who tell us contradictory things. We may believe the common myth that a big breakfast of animal fats, refined carbohydrates in the form of toast or heavily sugared cereals, dairy products, eggs and coffee is a top way to start the day. Lunch? Often its more fried food, refined carbohydrates and sugar. And whenever you're thirsty during the day, there's a plentiful supply of coffee, tea and soft drinks, or (if you're 'health conscious') fruit drinks full of sugar and preservatives.

It's part of the modern lifestyle that more and more meals are bought ready-made outside the home (in America, it's estimated that 50 per cent of all meals are now take-away, and England is follow-ing the trend) and the vast majority of this food is deep fried, heavily processed and full of salt, sugar and additives of all kinds. If you want to eat real food when you're away from home you may have to take your own, although this is changing as more and more people are requesting healthy take-away sandwiches and pure fruit and vegetable juices.

In Western society our fat consumption has increased by 30 per cent over the past two gener-ations. So have our fat-related illnesses.

We need about 900 milligrams of salt daily, but many of us currently eat about **fifteen times** that much. Although we need both sodium and chloride, the elements in common salt, as nutrients, the body finds it difficult to metabolise large amounts of the combination. Excess salt can cause fluid retention and high blood pressure in some people. Salt substitutes are generally not good dietary inclusions, but vegetables, and particularly vegetable juices, contain both sodium and chloride in forms which are easily assimilated by the body. People often crave salt, and this craving may be a signal that their diet is simply not supplying the minerals their bodies need.

Similarly, our consumption of refined white sugar is greatly excessive. Frequent doses of this nutritionally useless substance contribute to obesity, tooth decay and blood sugar disorders. Many of us are 'sugar junkies'; we crave the short-term lift which sugar gives us, but pay a long-term price for it.

Craving the food that kills us

But you've heard all this before. So why do so many of us find it so hard to avoid eating the things we know are slowly killing us? One compelling reason is that many of these substances are the very ones which create food tolerance/addiction, as described earlier.

To take a very common example, let's look at salt. We **should** have a good look at it, because unless we're actually taking steps to avoid it, we're eating much more of it than we were ever meant to.

It's not hard to understand why. Sodium, one of the components of salt, is essential to life. Throughout most of our revolutionary history, salt was scarce. Our kidneys are set up to conserve sodium and get rid of excess potassium, because there is little sodium and relatively large amounts of potassium in the traditional human diet of fruits and vegetables. To ensure that we'd make an effort to get the sodium we needed, we developed a taste for it. We sought it out.

Today, we've reversed the amounts of sodium and potassium we eat, but we still crave salt because our evolving biochemistry had no idea what the twentieth century was going to be like. Not only is salt no longer in short supply, it's impossible to avoid huge amounts of it if we eat prepared foods. It's added in copious quantities to almost everything except fresh foods.

One of the reasons why the food processing companies use so much of it in their products is because the processing removes most of the food's real flavour. Adding salt is a cheap way of making unnatural food substances taste like something worth eating. Another advantage for the manufacturers of adding salt to their products is that it hooks you on them. Like all addictive substances, the more you have, the more you want. That's why the high-profit, no-value snack foods are loaded with it. They're 'more-ish'. Whoever eats one chip, or one salted peanut?

A test on favourite snack foods carried out by the Howard Florey Institute on Experimental Physiology and Medicine at Melbourne University found that small packets of crisps, cheese 'things' or nuts (designed to be eaten by one person, and universally sold in school tuckshops as well as all the usual commercial outlets) contained between three and four *grams* of salt. Even adults need less than one gram a day; children, with their much smaller body weight, need correspondingly less.

So what's wrong with salt? It's linked with hypertension, strokes, kidney disease, heart ailments and obesity. It's a direct contributing factor in a very large number of deaths.

It's beyond the scope of this book to go into detail about how all the various components of the modern Western diet do their indisputable harm. Such information is readily available. As a person taking back responsibility for your own health and well-being, you owe yourself this knowledge. We are the ones who must make the changes, and clear information is a great help. One of the most thorough and interesting books on the subject is David A. Phillips *New Dimensions in Health: From Soil to Psyche*. Another is *Living Health*, by Harvey and Marilyn Diamond. And there are many more. So irrefutable is the evidence about the inherent inadequacy and long-term bad effects of a diet based on the Western staples of refined flour, sugar, salt, caffeine and fats that there's widespread agreement in this one area, at least.

The modern Western diet is a complex subject. It's connected to everything from the subtleties of body chemistry and human psychology to the marketing practices of international commercial conglomerates. Its implications made frightening and anger-inducing reading.

Fortunately, the rules of following a **good** diet are not complicated at all. This is especially true now that, due to modern commercial techniques, a wonderful variety of fresh, whole foods is available all year round at reasonable prices. **The ideal diet for permanent cleansing and optimal nutrition is simple, inexpensive, easy to follow and satisfying.**

Food combining

The cleansing diet acknowledges both common sense and one very fundamental principle: food combining. Digestion is a series of chemical transformations, triggered by the catalytic action of enzymes. If you mix a number of foods with very different properties together — and that's what you're doing whenever you eat a miscellany of foods of varying acidity and alkalinity — you're creating real difficulties for your stomach.

The stomach can only effectively handle one single chemical reaction at a time. This probably reflects our long human history as hunter/gatherers, when eating a single food at a time (and each one containing the enzymes necessary for its own digestion) was normal eating practice.

Faced with the simultaneous and incompatible demands of meals comprising literally everything 'from soup to nuts', the stomach does its best. It complains a little, in the form of indigestion. As time goes on, people who ignore these complaints may develop gastric ulcers, colitis, bowel cancer or a host of other serious disturbances of the digestive tract.

Luckily, they're avoidable disturbances. When you understand how the process works and adopt a sensible manner of eating, you won't have digestive problems. You also won't have an excessively acid internal state of affairs, which can lead to arthritis or gout. You won't develop osteoporosis due to a highly acidic diet leaching calcium from your body. You'll have much less chance of developing cancer, heart disease, or any other degenerative disorder. Allergies will be reduced. Constipation and bowel cancer due to lack of fibre are less likely, as are varicose veins, gallstones, obesity and high blood pressure. Your teeth will be stronger, your nerves steadier and your energy higher.

The simple basic rules of the optimal human diet

1   Eat foods singly, or in combinations which are compatible in their digestive requirements (see below).

2   Eat only fruit in the morning. You don't need a heavy breakfast. Fruit is quickly and easily digested, stimulates the proper functioning of the entire system and contains rich amounts of enzymes, natural sugars and pure water. It requires almost no preparation, and it's delicious.

3   For lunch, a mixed salad or salad-starch combination, like a salad sandwich, is good. Make your own bread or use Pritikin bread. The starch could also be obtained from such foods as rice, corn, millet, beans, potato, lentils and pumpkin. A full list of the food groups is given on pages 123–5.

4   For dinner, a salad or vegetables with a protein food. Allow plenty of time before going to bed for the protein to be digested (it can take up to four hours).

5   Feel free to switch around the lunch/dinner suggestions.

6   Eat as low on the food chain as possible. This means choosing whole fruits, vegetables and whole grains. Such a diet helps you to avoid high concentrations of fats, pesticides and synthetic hormones, as well as giving you the great nutritional benefits of whole foods.

7   Clean all food which is subjected to spraying, especially fruits. An effective way to remove the residue of chemical sprays is to use an organic detergent to wash the fruit.

8   Eat organically-grown foods whenever you can get them. They're becoming more readily available and the more we buy them, the more we encourage the growers to provide more.

9   Avoid the killers: alcohol, excessive salt, refined flour and sugar, processed foods and foods which are artificially coloured, flavoured, puffed, fluffed, stuffed, stabilised, energised, deodorised and all the rest of it. If you buy something in a box, read the label! To paraphrase Sir Macfarlane Burnet, 'If in doubt, don't eat it!'

10   About three-quarters of your diet should consist of fruit and vegetables; eat these raw as much as possible. The remainder of the diet is made up of concentrated protein foods, carbohydrates and fats.

11   Don't drink juice or water with your meal.

12   Eat when you're hungry, and not simply from habit.

Basic food combining rules

1   Don't combine proteins and starches in the same meal. Yes, I know it's the basis of most schools of cooking — meat and potatoes, macaroni and cheese, rice and satay chicken. But we've broken with other traditional beliefs and practices following our increased knowledge, and we need to break with this one, too.

2   Vegetables combine well with both proteins and starches. This combination should form the basis

of most of your meals, except for breakfast.

3 Acid and sub-acid fruits go well together; the combination of either with sweet fruits is less desirable. See the complete lists of food groups below.

4 Starches and fruit are not a good combination.

5 Melons should be eaten on their own. They are the easiest of all foods to digest and pass quickly through the stomach. They're ideal for breakfast.

6 The wonderful avocado goes with everything, and is one of the best foods you can eat. Take advantage of this wonderful fruit when it is available in the shops.

7 All juices can be mixed because they're absorbed by the body at about the same rate.

And that's it, in simple terms. More detailed information about food combining is available from natural health centres, and in a number of publications (see Bibliography).

The Basic Food Groups

proteins	starches
cheese	beans
eggs	buckwheat
fish	chestnuts
meat	chick peas
nuts	corn
poultry	lentils
seeds	millet
yoghurt	millet
	oats
	potatoes
	pumpkin
	rice
	rye
	wheat

vegetables

asparagus
beetroot
broccoli
cabbage
capsicum
carrots
cauliflower
celery
cucumber
eggplant
fresh beans
fresh peas
globe artichokes
herbs
lettuce
parsley
silverbeet
sprouts
squash
tomatoes
turnip
zucchini

acid fruits

grapefruit
lemons
limes
oranges
passionfruit
pineapple
plums
pomegranate
strawberries

sub-acid fruits

apples
apricots
blackberries
blackcurrants
cherries
fresh figs
grapes
guavas
mangoes
mulberries
paw paws
peaches
pears
raspberries

fats
avocadoes
butter
coconut
seed oils

melons
honeydew
rockmelon
watermelon

sweet fruits
bananas
custard apples
persimmon
raisins, dates and
   all dried fruits

12 *STOP!*
Saving the Only Planet We Have

'The major advances in civilisation are processes that all but wreck the societies in which they occur.'

Alfred North Whitehead

Never has the truth of Alfred North Whitehead's observation been so clear as it is today. Even the most determined ostrich can see the end result of the past two generations' eager, uninformed collusion with the hard-sell tactics underpinning the industrialised consumer society.

It's a society which has made a **few** of us in the world very rich at the expense of **most** other people and **all** other life forms. Individual species, each one a unique and irreplaceable expression of this planet's life, are presently disappearing — becoming extinct — at the rate of three every day; forests are being sacrificed to feed an insatiable hunger for paper, wood products and grazing land for cattle; starvation is growing as fast as the world debt and the oceans are full of garbage. Our streams, rivers and lakes are dying. Our croplands are poisoned by chemicals and salt. And the air in our cities has sometimes become literally unfit to breathe.

The only encouraging aspect is that you really can't fool all of the people all of the time. More and more of us are starting to respond like any sensible creature does when it's under a grave threat; we're looking for alternatives that will preserve us.

Air, the basis of life

The very basis of life is air. We can go without food for a long time. We can survive without water for a little while. But without air, we're dead in a matter of minutes. In an average lifetime, a person takes about 500 million breaths. We take air for granted. It's just **there**. Our first independent breath marks our entry into life and our last one signifies our exit from it.

Most people in the world today live in cities, where the air is heavily contaminated with particles of carbon and other irritants. It's laden with carbon monoxide, sulphuric acid, hydrochloric acid, nitric acid, hydrocyanic acid, lead, benzene, methane, ammonia and a host of other lethal substances. We've come to accept it, like the boiling frog, because it happened gradually. And besides, what can we do about it? You can't stop progress! That's what we've been told all our lives.

In the short term, there **isn't** much we can do. Only a determined grass-roots protest to enforce strict controls on car emissions and industrial pollution, and to reverse the insane destruction of the forests which clean the poisons from our air, is going to make a difference in the long run. For most people, moving away from sources of air pollution is not an option.

This is one area where it is extremely difficult to protect ourselves effectively. Urban air has high lead levels, mainly from car exhausts, and even tiny amounts of lead interfere with the metabolism of haemoglobin. Lead damages brain cells, bones and kidneys. It's a major cause of mental retardation in children.

Following the cleansing diet helps to detoxify the body in general, and to strengthen your resistance to the poisoning. Air conditioners are not an answer, as they cause more problems than they solve due to the cooling agents used in them and their suscep-tibility to bacterial contamination. You still need fresh air, especially while sleeping, and in spite of the pol-lution of most urban air your bedroom windows should be open at night, unless you live directly on a busy road.

Some people find air ionisers a distinct help in ridding indoor environments of pollens, smoke and dust. Others don't. If you are particularly sensitive to such substances, they may be worth a try.

If you live near a busy thoroughfare (and even if you don't) plant as many fast-growing trees as your space allows. They're your best defence against dirty air.

The same is true inside the house. In conducting research into biological methods of purifying the air in space stations, American scientists found that old-fashioned pot plants were remarkably efficient in absorbing common harmful gases (formaldehyde, benzene, carbon monoxide and nitrous oxide) from the air. Gerbera daisies, ficus and crysanthemums all did a good job, but the top performer, the most effective in removing harmful air pollutants, was the humble philodendron. So enjoy the many benefits of surrounding yourself with living plants, especial-ly if you live in a flat with no access to a garden. And when you have a day or two off, enjoy yourself as much as possible in clean air. Go out in the bush,

climb a mountain, walk along the seashore, ride a
bike in the park. Even **some** fresh air is better than
none.

If you work in a building with sealed windows and
a closed ventilation system, you could try complain-
ing. It's not humane and it's not reasonable to be en-
capsulated in a glass, cement and plastic cocoon. At
the very least, suggest that some big, healthy, broad-
leaved plants be installed in your work area, or bring
them in yourself. You'll have to rotate them, because
they won't thrive for long in such an environment.

Water, a fundamental necessity

Water is the second most fundamental human neces-
sity. Here you have a larger measure of control over
what goes into your body. And that's fortunate,
because urban water supplies are treated with
chlorine to kill bacteria, fluoride to decrease tooth
decay, and contaminated with soap, oil, copper,
arsenic, pesticides, fertilisers and many inorganic
minerals. Chlorine is a deadly poison, implicated in
heart disease and proven to destroy the body's
reserves of vitamin E. But at least its role in reducing
bacterial illness in the population is unquestionable.

Not so fluoride. This potent toxin has **not** been
clearly proven to reduce tooth decay at all. Even if
it did, the ethics of involuntarily medicating the entire
population with such a dangerous substance are certainly open to debate. The official chemical register,
the *Merck Index*, describes fluoride as follows:

> *Human toxicity*: Severe symptoms from ingestion
> of less than 1 gram; death from 5 to 10 grams.
> *Sublethal*: Nausea and vomiting, abdominal distress,
> diarrhoea, stupor, weakness. *Lethal*: muscular weak-

ness, tremors, convulsions, collapse, respiratory and cardiac failure, death. *Chronic*: mottling of tooth enamel, osteosclerosis.

Use: An insecticide, particularly for roaches and ants; other pesticide formulations; as a steel degassing agent; in electroplating; frosting glass; in the flouridation of drinking water; manufacture of coated paper.

The fact that the supply of this potent toxin can't be completely regulated, and that it's a cumulative substance in the human body, should be enough reason not to use it. However, if you live in a city, you are subjected to its dubious benefits in your drinking water, whether you want it or not.

If you **don't** want it, there are a number of water purifiers on the market which will remove it. They will also, at varying levels of effectiveness, remove the other added chemicals, bacteria, detergents, pesticides, lead, and nitrates.

The Australian Consumer's Association recently tested available water purifiers and rated them according to their cost, flow rate and effectiveness at getting rid of various contaminants. There was considerable variety in the results but some of the carbon filtration units and ion exchange models performed quite well. The more expensive reverse osmosis types were the most effective in removing a wide range of impurities, but about five litres of tap water are needed to produce one litre of clean water using this method. Over a year, that's a lot of wasted water so if you use one of these, it would be a good idea to find a way of putting that overflow to use. Distillation units were effective but relatively slow, and they require electricity to run.

You need to inform yourself of the various advantages and drawbacks of the different systems before you choose one. If you live alone, or can afford it, it may be preferable to buy distilled water for drinking.

By following the cleansing diet, a good deal of your water will be consumed in the purest possible form — that of fresh fruits and vegetables.

We must stop adding to the problem

Since it's a universal law that the microcosm reflects the macrocosm, what you do as an individual always reflects back to the surrounding environment. By deciding not to eat rubbishy foods, for example, you make a choice which affects not only your personal health but the health of the planet. If enough of us stop buying refined and processed foods, more healthy alternatives will be offered to us. If we refrain from putting every separate vegetable and fruit into its own plastic bag, the earth and its oceans will benefit. Plastic **never** breaks down; the bags and rings of the throwaway society of the past two decades will still be in the ocean, killing seals and dolphins, thousands of years from now.

But we can stop adding to the problem, and we must. 'They' will continue to manufacture polluting products as long as **we** continue to make it profitable for them. It's up to us to break the cycle.

So have a good look around your home environment. And while you're doing so, have a look at your ideas about what should or shouldn't be there. Most of us have accepted the conditioning of Western scientific philosophy, based on the false premise that humans are somehow separate from the rest of life;

that we are the only species which is exempt from natural processes and natural law.

It's a very dangerous delusion.

Dealing with unwanted creatures

One outcome of this delusion is the belief that no other life form should share our immediate environment unless, like a pot plant or a canary, we put it there ourselves. Millions of advertising dollars emphasise the undesirability or downright dirtiness of all insects, no matter how harmless or even beneficial they may be. It's true that our introduction of cows and sheep into an environment that was never meant to support them has resulted in an oversupply of flies; it's true that modern cities seem designed to benefit the multiplication of cockroaches, fleas, ants and silverfish. There are therefore times and situations in which, for comfort and hygiene, controls must be applied.

The emphasis, however, should be on exactly that: control. **Not** eradication, **not** spraying indiscriminate poisons around our homes to contaminate the air we breathe and the surfaces we touch. Because there's nothing yet designed which is capable of killing **some** living organisms while leaving everything else unharmed. We share the same genetic reservoir as our diminutive 'enemies'. Whenever we poison them, we poison ourselves as well.

Probably the first thing to do is to develop some tolerance and understanding of how we all fit together. Many of the insects who share our space are harmless, temporary visitors who need no response from us at all. The few who must be controlled can be handled in effective but relatively non-polluting ways.

Rule number one: no sprays. There are several reasons for this. The propellant in the can may well contain chlorofluorocarbons, which are destroying the earth's ozone layer. **Never** use them. Secondly, you and everyone around you will breathe them in, and they're a vile toxic mix for **any** life form. Both the production and the use of poison sprays are extremely hard on the planet.

The best defence against unwanted creatures is prevention. Use fly screens and mosquito nets. Make sure your doors and windows fit well. Seal up cracks where insects come in. Clean out your pet's water bowl instead of just topping it up. Keep a clean house by putting your grains and foodstuffs in tightly-stoppered jars. Vacuum frequently. When cockroaches, mice, flies and fleas have nowhere to hide and little to eat, they'll quickly desert your house for a more compatible environment.

Many bothersome insects dislike lavender, tansy and pennyroyal. A pot of these herbs near your door can work wonders in discouraging insects. Plant them if you have a garden, or have a big pot of French lavender in your flat. If you have a dog or cat, put pennyroyal near their sleeping place or use pennyroyal oil as a flea deterrent on their fur. Lavender in the clothes closet will make your clothes smell lovely, and will definitely discourage destructive moths. A lavender pot-pourri near the door will let mosquitoes know they're better off elsewhere.

When you need to take sterner measures, try to use mechanics instead of chemistry. If your pet has presentedyou with a problem of galloping fleas, **vacuum**! Even if you gas your pet (and yourself) with chemicals, you'll still have more fleas when the eggs hatch later on. Vacuuming regularly gets rid of them.

Use old-fashioned sticky strips for flies. It's far less poisonous to you than sprays, and although unsightly, it's effective. You're killing things, and you may as well accept it. Sticky paper loaded with dead flies is far less harmful to you, and to everything else, than spraying toxic poisons into the air.

For mice and rats, use traps. Again, you are killing things; why not do it in a clean way? Rodent poisons are extremely strong, extremely toxic and if you must get rid of vermin, why not do it without harming everything else in the immediate environment?

If these measures are not enough, use dry, powdered and specific remedies that don't kill indiscriminately. Use organic substances that break down quickly and don't linger to poison you over a long period of time.

For cockroaches, put a half-and-half mixture of borax and icing sugar or borax and honey in a jar with vaseline-coated sides in your cupboards and under the sink. Some Vick's Vaporub around cracks and doors will help. You can dust dark, damp breeding places with diatomaceous earth. Stop up cracks around drainage pipes, and seal any crevices where the beasties are coming in. Keep your kitchen clean. Line drawers and shelves with paper. Use close-fitting lids on foods and garbage receptacles.

For silverfish, frequent vacuuming of floors and bookshelves is the most effective method of control. If you're fortunate enough to attract a big huntsman spider to your premises, thank your lucky stars. It will seek out and eat as many of these as it can find, and then graciously disappear without you having to do a thing about it. If you haven't got a huntsman, dried or fresh bay leaves discourage silverfish, and so does pennyroyal.

For mozzies, get rid of any possible breeding places, like stagnant pools of water; pets' dirty water bowls, and wet garden areas. Garlic spray, penny-royal and lavender oil are good repellents. Again, tight-fitting screens are your best prevention.

The same is true for flies. In addition, close off your chimney in warm weather, because this is a favourite place of entry for flies. Some mint or basil growing in pots near the door, either inside or out, will also discourage them. And if all else fails, the old-fashioned fly swatter is both effective and non-polluting.

Poison sprays

You should completely forego the dubious effective-ness of poison spray. Shell Pestrips and their ilk contain dichloros, a highly toxic organophosphate which is a proven human carcinogen. So do com-mercial flea collars for pets. Avoid them like the plague, because that's exactly what they are. All organophosphates destroy the enzyme choline-sterase, which regulates your central nervous system. You can't afford to destroy it. It bears repeating: any poisonous substance capable of killing other life forms is **not good for you**.

Although very few of the active ingredients in pesticides can be shown to be harmless to humans, the use of these substances is increasing year by year. Fewer than 5 per cent of the nearly 50 000 pesticide formulations produced in the USA have been properly tested. Even so, some of these poisons have been shown to have drastic effects on human health. All too often, even when these substances are banned for use in the UK or the USA, they continue to be exported for use in Third World countries.

World production of pesticides is currently about 3 000 000 tonnes per year. In the UK, approximately 4.5 million litres are annually sprayed on crops. They contaminate groundwater and river systems, indiscriminately killing fish, frogs and beneficial insects.

The claim that food production would drop drastically without the use of pesticides has been shown in recent years to be completely untrue. Their widespread use simply creates ever-greater pest infestations as the target species become resistant, and their natural predators are wiped out by scattergun use of these substances.

Most pesticides are synthetic organic chemicals, and include a number of known carcinogens. These substances become increasingly concentrated as they move up the food chain, so that mammals (like us) end up with significant residues in our fatty tissues. We are gradually poisoning ourselves, *en masse*; this seems an odd behaviour for a supposedly intelligent species to engage in.

13 *Cleaning Up Our Act*

'It's not the size of the ship, it's the size of the waves.'
Little Richard

We've talked about the need to avoid taking unnecessary medical drugs. What about the other drugs so many of us use? Poisoning our inner environment forms the basis of much social interaction and it can be hard to avoid. No one today is unaware of the dangers of the legal drugs, tobacco and alcohol, but young people (and especially young women) continue to take up smoking as a habit in spite of much greater public awareness of its dangers. And the trend toward an increasing regular consumption of alcohol shows no signs of diminishing.

So much has been written about the personal and social costs of these two substances that there's no need to dwell on them here. But it's worth noting that of all drug-related deaths in the Western world (excluding medical drugs), the great majority are due to tobacco (80 per cent) and alcohol (nearly 20 per cent) and only 3 or 4 per cent can be linked to illegal drugs. Alcohol takes a particularly high toll on people under thirty-five, being a factor in many of the motor vehicle accidents which account for three-quarters of the deaths in this age group.

You certainly wouldn't guess this by reading the papers. We focus most of our concern about drugs on the relatively minor killers and elevate the manufacturers of alcohol to the status of millionaire cultural heroes.

Drinking alcohol in very moderate amounts may not harm you, but there's no way to make smoking, either active or passive, safe.

Pollutants at home

Less obvious sources of indoor pollution are the many household products which are made from by-products of petrochemical hydrocarbons. Synthetic materials in furniture, cars and offices all emit or 'outgas' substances to which many people are allergic. Gas stoves and heaters, aerosol sprays, paint, lacquer, air fresheners, hair spray, oven cleaners, detergents, waxes, bleaches and many cosmetics all contribute to the creation of a toxic, highly allergenic environment in the home.

Gas, formaldehyde and plastics are the worst offenders. Many people experience symptoms of nausea, headache and chronic fatigue due to leaks from badly fitting gas connections or just from the fumes from the gas appliances themselves, which contain carbon monoxide and nitrogen dioxide. If you have to use a gas cooker, an exhaust fan above it helps get rid of the toxic fumes.

Gas space heaters are major polluters of your home, and so are open-flame oil and kerosene heaters. The air that fuels the flame is full of suspended matter and molecules of various ambient chemicals which, when burned with the fuel, can form highly dangerous compounds. Since a room with such a heater is usually tightly sealed against the fresh air in order to obtain maximum heat, the ill effects are increased.

A very common chemical found in the home is formaldehyde, which is manufactured from petroleum products. Major sources are petrol and diesel engines, backyard incinerators, insulation, rat poison, insecticides, air deoderants, toothpastes, shampoos, mouthwash, plywood and particle board, fur and leather goods, newsprint, latex paint, glues, many fabrics and most fabric-treatment products. Common reactions to excessive formaldehyde include memory loss, depression, fatigue, dermatitis, respiratory ailments and headache.

To decrease your exposure to this chemical, you can wash new clothes and bedding in borax or add ordinary vinegar to the rinse water. Use plants as your air fresheners and avoid backyard burning, even if your local council still permits it.

Synthetic curtains and carpets are full of chemicals which release slowly into the air. The ones backed with latex glue and rubber, polyester or PVC are the worst. A woven wool or wool/nylon carpet without synthetic backing, or a bare wooden floor, is preferable.

Even natural clothing fibres like cotton and wool are generally bleached, treated with caustic alkalis, coated with starches and gums and moth-proofed, sometimes with dieldrin. Many people are highly sensitive to these substances, and to all the chemicals used in washing and treating fabrics. Dry-cleaning solvents are the most potent of all, and are related to the dangerous chlorofluoromethanes used in refrigerators, air conditioners and as aerosol propellants.

Effective organic cleansers

Highly toxic household cleansers can be avoided altogether. They're bad for your skin and your respiratory system and when you wash them down the sink, they pollute the waterways. There are effective organic substitutes for the whole dazzling range of cleansers and detergents on the supermarket shelf. And they're cheaper, because you're not paying for the fancy packaging and the massive advertising campaigns designed to get you to buy them.

For surface cleaning of windows and floors, just use a solution of vinegar in warm water. If scouring is needed, use bicarbonate of soda. Borax whitens fabrics without harming them and doesn't pollute the water supply. For the washing up, bicarbonate of soda or a *small* amount of biodegradable liquid detergent is enough. Blocked drains can be opened with a cup of hot water followed by half a cup of borax. Again, use mechanics instead of chemistry wherever you can; a small plunger works as well as lye, and doesn't poison anything.

Most detergents are not plain soap but chemical brews of foam boosters, cheap synthetic perfumes, brighteners and enzymes. Since they all end up in our waterways, they're bad news. You can use plain soaps or biodegradable detergents, and save money by avoiding unnecessary additives like fabric softeners and stain removers. Your wash will be cleaner, and so will the earth.

For personal hygiene, following a cleansing diet is the best way to make your breath sweet and your body odour unobjectionable. A warm bath or shower and the use of pure coconut oil soap is all the extra cleansing you need. An effective aid to all-over cleanliness and softer skin is the use of a dry skin brush. This is any medium soft natural bristle brush; simply brush your skin with it for a few minutes before your bath or shower. It removes dead cells and impurities and stimulates the natural cleansing ability of your skin. It feels good and leaves you glowing.

You don't need toothpaste at all. You can clean your teeth just as effectively by brushing with a soft brush and water, and using dental floss to remove plaque. If you can't break the toothpaste habit, shop for one of the non-chemical types and use very little.

Avoid mercury and aluminium

Two poisons you should do everything possible to avoid are mercury and aluminium. The expression 'mad as a hatter' stems from mercury's effect on human beings; mercury compounds were traditionally used in working felt for hats. The dumping of mercury waste into Minimata Bay by a Japanese plastics factory in the 1950s killed or seriously disabled more than 100 people. Hundreds of people were poisoned in Iraq, Pakistan and Guatemala when they ate seed-grains which had been treated with methyl mercury fungicides.

Today we ingest mercury from fish, pesticides, industrial factories which use chlorine, pulp mills, some latex paints, fabric softeners, floor waxes and polishes, air-conditioning filters, some batteries, wood preservatives and lawn fungicides.

Once in the body, mercury accumulates and binds itself to the cell membranes. It affects the function of the kidneys by blocking enzymes and it can cross the placental barrier to cause chromosomal damage and irreversible mental retardation.

There are about 20 000 tonnes of mercury compounds released into the world's environment every year. The oceans now contain an estimated 70 million tonnes.

Many people who avoid eating small coastal fish and shellfish because they're aware of their mercury content believe it's safe to consume larger, deep sea fish. If anything, the concentration of mercury may be higher in the larger fish because, as they eat the smaller ones, the level accumulates at each step in the food chain.

Aluminium, another substance to avoid as much as possible, is even more pervasive than mercury. Household sources include baking powder, antacids, deodorants (some contain as much as 24 per cent aluminium compounds), aluminium foil, cans, beer, milk, pickles (where alum is used in the pickling process), toothpaste, nasal sprays, food colours, table salt, bleached flour, insulated cables and wires, pesticides and fumigant residues in food.

Aluminium has been linked to emphysema, liver and kidney dysfunction and senile dementia (Alzheimer's disease). Since aluminium breaks down in contact with both acids and alkalis it gets transferred to you in the food, and should therefore never be used for cooking utensils. Most European countries don't permit the sale of aluminium pots and pans at all.

Bleached and self-raising flours all contain aluminium, so buy plain wholewheat flour and substitute beaten egg whites or a mixture of baking soda and cream of tartar for baking powder. Use sea salt, and wrap food in plain paper instead of aluminium foil. Check the labels on suspect products and choose alternatives when aluminium or one of its compounds is included.

Controlling garden pests

In the garden, don't use poisons and chemical fertilisers. Your organic mulch from composting will put the necessary nutrients back into the soil, and sprays made from organic substances like garlic are highly effective in controlling pests. So are birds. A feeder table out of the reach of cats is good insurance against caterpillars and other unwelcome visitors. Soapy water sprays on leaves deters many insects, as does a good blast of clean water with the hose. Snails can be trapped with a little beer in the bottom of a glass jar.

There are many excellent books available on organic gardening methods. Any other way of growing plants depletes the soil and poisons beneficial insects like bees and earthworms along with the 'pests'. The idea is to work **with** nature, not against it.

The same principle holds true in every area. Every suggestion in this book is based on a single premise; we have created an adverse environment for ourselves in many ways and we need to know how to cooperate with ourselves in order to correct it. By truly nourishing ourselves we give back as well as take; by respecting ourselves it follows that we also respect our home, this earth.

It's really not so hard. It's just a mixture of common sense, a little knowledge, and the determination to live in a clean and loving way with all the other living things around us.

14 *Being Your Own Healer*

'Innumerable confusions and a feeling of despair invariably emerge in periods of great technological and cultural transition.'

Marshall McLuhan

In the Australian film *The Bounty* starring Mel Gibson, there's a scene in which the mutineers, having decided that the Tahitian world of love, freedom and enjoyment of nature was better than anything eighteenth-century England had to offer them, start shooting the playful dolphins around their ship 'for fun'. Nothing could more clearly illustrate the essential dilemma of our conflicting response to personal liberation. We may want freedom and power in our own lives; we may take real steps to achieve it; and we may then sabotage our own growth because of old programming which tells us things like 'what you do won't make any difference anyway' and 'you don't deserve to be healthy, happy and loved'.

A wealth of literature now exists which goes deeply into the causes of personal feelings of disempowerment, and offers techniques and ideas for overcoming self-destructive modes of thought. All the various writers are in agreement on one fundamental issue. Our thoughts determine our emotional reactions, and these in turn have a profound effect on our physical health, our levels of satisfaction in our work, and the quality of our relationships.

Coping with stress

We're all familiar with the basic concept of stress. Dr Hans Selye, who is Director of the Institute of Experimental Medicine and Surgery at the University of Montreal, has exhaustively researched the way our bodies respond to stress. Dr Selye defines stress as 'the non-specific response of the body to any demand made on it' and described the process of activation of the stress response and the body's readjustment or adaption to the new situation created by the stressor.

Stress is not the problem. It becomes a problem only when our adaptation is too intense or unpleasant. This occurs when the demands made on us are beyond our ability to cope with them. We get out of balance. Distress may also occur when the demands made on us are **less** than what we need. Boring, repetitive work, for instance, or unemployment, can cause an overload of stress because we're not being challenged as much as we need to be.

Our ability to cope with stress adequately is influenced by the total amount of stress in our lives and the state of our inner resources. This is in turn determined by the adequacy of our diet, the level of fatigue we're living with, and our emotional reserves. A demand you may welcome at one time can be the last straw under different conditions.

Many of us live with a constant level of stress which is close to our crisis point. If our bodies contain a high level of toxins, if we are chronically fatigued, we are under extreme stress. Any extra problem that comes along sends us over the top. We can't cope. We get sick, or we have an emotional outburst. We get into conflict with others. We have an accident.

We turn to pills or alcohol for 'help'.

Avoidance of stress is not the issue, because the stress reaction is an essential bodily process which keeps our adrenal system operating effectively. A chronic overload, however, leads to malfunction and to degenerative diseases. It's cumulative. During a long overstressed period, the body's immune response is suppressed, which is why you are so much more susceptible to illness and infection at such times.

You can reduce the amount of stress coming in, and you can also strengthen your ability to cope with it, in various ways.

Nutrition is a key factor in your ability to handle stress effectively, of course. A basically poor diet like the one eaten by most Westerners is severely stressful in itself, and drastically lowers your reserves of inner strength. All toxins create biological stress, but so do negative attitudes and a pessimistic world view. Chronic frustration, for example, is a constant state of low-level anger and it affects the body's integrity just as badly as a faulty diet or an overload of chemicals. Low self-esteem is another common, potent stressor. Only a conscious decision to change these things will help in the long run.

Toynbee observed that civilisations decline because of an internal hardening of ideas. The society becomes rigid and unable to respond creatively and spontaneously to its challenges. Exactly the same thing happens at an individual level when we retreat from necessary change into apathy or cynicism. Creativity and flexibility are necessary if we really want to **live** and not just exist.

A number of medical researchers have demonstrated conclusively that some foods alter the neurotransmitter levels in the brain. These control the signals which pass between the brain cells, and have a direct effect on mood and behaviour. Lead pollution and food additives are particularly damaging to your peace of mind because they have such a destructive effect on this process. Any food or chemical to which you are intolerant/addicted upsets the nervous system and can lead to mood swings, irritability, depression, insomnia, confusion and a drastically lowered stress threshold.

Dr Emanuel Cheraskin, Chairman of the Department of Oral Medicine at the University of Alabama, is one of the medical researchers who has studied the relationship between food and mood in depth. He found an undeniable correlation between nutrition and depression, accidents, antisocial behaviour, alcoholism, learning difficulties and behavioural problems in children, mental retardation and senility. Specifically, these symptoms are much more common among people whose basic diet consists of highly refined and processed foods, especially white sugar and flour.

Dr Richard Mackarness is another source of good information on this subject, and so is clinical ecologist Dr David R. Collison. Their books make fascinating reading, and they also make good sense.

Having established that a good basic diet is essential to coping effectively with stress, let's look at some of the other resources which can make the difference between living a healthy and fulfilling life, and just coping. Or *not* coping.

Many people turn to mood-altering drugs when they feel overwhelmed by their lives. If you decide you really must use them, ensure that it's only a temporary situation — just a short respite to allow you to have a good look at what's causing the stress, and to do something about changing it. Such drugs can never provide a permanent way of coping because they're addictive, and they end up increasing the very symptoms of distress you're probably taking them to alleviate. Panic attacks, phobias, and insomnia all return with extra force after a period of time on drugs like Serepax, Mogadon and Valium. Withdrawal from them can be horrendous.

If you are experiencing a crisis due to stress, seize on it as a clear message of concern for you from your inner healer, and use it as an opportunity for positive change. The first element in the process of using stress constructively is to have a good look at your life and identify the major causes of the overload you're experiencing. What can you do about them? Work on what's possible.

The importance of relaxation

At the same time, learn a simple physical relaxation technique and use it. Since it's impossible to be relaxed and tense at the same time, your physical intervention and control breaks the vicious cycle in increasing tension.

The process of releasing body tension is a direct way to let go and create an inner atmosphere of deep rest. There are many classes and courses where you can learn and practice the method, or there are progressive relaxation tapes you can buy and play at home. Half an hour of such practice every day will make an enormous difference in your life. John Mason's *Guide to Stress Reduction* is an excellent source of a number of effective relaxation techniques.

Once you have mastered the basic process (and it's not hard) you'll be able to use the method any time you need it. While you're driving, talking on the telephone, doing any sort of non-demanding work, you can also be practising the conscious relaxation of parts of the body and letting go of tension with each breath. Your blood pressure, heart rate, breathing, and the release of adrenalin into the bloodstream all decrease whenever you relax. It leaves you feeling balanced, clear, and better able to cope with the demands that are made upon you.

Closely connected with the progressive relaxation method is the use of imaginative visualisation. By combining this technique with deep rest you will greatly aid your inner healer in its task of keeping you healthy and happy. The use of colour imagery, mental enjoyment of beautiful places and various auto-suggestive techniques empower the life force enormously. Louise Hay's books and tapes provide a rich resource of this material, as does Shakti Gawain's *Creative Visualization*.

Louise Hay's book *You Can Heal Your Life* and John Harrison's *Love Your Disease: It's Keeping You Healthy* are both based on the awareness that disease plays an important symbolic role in our lives. We don't get cancer or heart disease by accident; we choose the form our distress will take for reasons which make sense, given our family background and the ideas we've accepted as a basic world view. By coming to an understanding of our inner process, we can not only heal ourselves but be immeasurably enriched by the various opportunities for change provided by our lives. Our own ideas, and especially the ones we constantly reinforce as we talk to ourselves mentally, create our experiences in the world. This is not a matter of blaming the victim or being uncompassionate. It's simply acknowledging that each of us creates the conditions of our own life, and that, if we want to, we have enormous power to change them.

Changing your reality for the better

Over the years I've found a few powerful ideas that really work in terms of changing my reality for the better. They come from various sources and experiences: perhaps some of them will resonate with you. Take whatever ideas you can use and develop them for yourself.

- I have a centre of wisdom within me. It is always there and it always has been there. When I'm ready to grow, this centre will unfailingly attract the people and experiences I need into my life. It will also make sure that I take from these people only what I need; nothing else.

- My body, my health, my relationships, my work, my financial situation — everything in my life — mirror my own inner dialogue. This inner dialogue is composed of the things I tell myself, that is, the things I believe about myself and others.

- Treating the **symptoms** of a situation (whether it's a disease, or lack of money, or a bad relationship) only works temporarily. Unless I treat the **cause**, I'll just recreate the same situation again. I need to treat the cause, which is what I think and say.

- What I believe about myself and others becomes true for me.

- What I believe about myself, and about life, was

originally learned from the people who cared for me as a baby and a young child. They couldn't teach me anything they didn't know themselves. So if my mother, for example, did not love herself, she couldn't teach me to love myself. If she was afraid, or angry, or resentful, these attitudes and beliefs were passed on to me. This is not her fault. Our parents and guardians did the best they could, given what they themselves had been taught. We are victims of victims.

- But we don't have to stay victims. **The present is the point of power**. We can always choose, in the present, to change our negative beliefs.

- When we become aware of this, we realise that what we choose to believe right now is creating our future. I can have the future I want if I learn to be aware of what I'm thinking, and replace any negative or limiting beliefs with others which will support the life I really want.

- The first step is to become aware of what I **do** think. Some of us are so out of touch with our thoughts that we don't even realise something is wrong until we get sick, or have an accident, or a disastrous relationship. Even then we may feel it was caused by something external, and not created by our own beliefs. Other people may certainly behave badly, but what did I do to attract such people into my life?

- Our experiences all arise from our inner dialogue. Therefore, if we change our thoughts, we will have different feelings and different experiences.

- The most damaging thought patterns we can have are those of **resentment, criticism** (of both ourselves and others), **guilt** over the past and **fear** of the future. These four things handicap us and lead us to blame ourselves and others, rather than change. 'I don't deserve good things' and 'I'm just not good enough' are real killers.

- An excellent first step in changing negative patterns is to repeat the affirmation again and again that '**I am now willing to release the pattern in me that has created this problem**'. Use this affirmation and put in the specific thing you want to change, for example, 'I am now willing to release the pattern in me which has prevented me from finding a wonderful, supportive lover' or 'I am now willing to release the pattern in me which has made me overweight'.

- By practising this affirmation (and it's more effective if you look at yourself in the mirror while you say it out loud) we are giving up the role of victim, and beginning to take back our power in the situation.

- We need to release outmoded ideas and beliefs which do not nourish and support us. Our ideas about life and about ourselves should always support what is good for us.

- The fundamental problems in people's lives are always only **one** problem: lack of self-love. Bad relationships, stifled creativity and physical disease are all results of our lack of self-love.

- When we begin to consciously love and approve of ourselves, all these things improve.

- Many of us have been influenced by the illogical belief that being hard on ourselves is a good thing; that it is virtuous, somehow, to disapprove of ourselves. This is pretty silly when you think about it. If we find it hard to give ourselves love and approval, we are still influenced by the old limiting ideas which someone taught us long ago, when we were too little to think for ourselves. Usually these limiting beliefs came from people who weren't making their own lives work very well.

• Luckily, limiting beliefs are just thoughts. I can change them whenever I choose.

Some initial steps

1 **Never, ever** criticise yourself. Self-criticism locks us into the negative patterns. Anger at ourselves locks us in really tightly. Understand and be gentle with yourself. Have compassion. Self-acceptance and self approval **right now** is the key to change. A thousand times a day say 'I love and approve of myself'. Say it while you're walking along the street, driving a car, or drifting off to sleep. It will become a new automatic thought, replacing old ones like 'I can't do it' of 'What if this or that happens?' or 'What's the point anyway?'

2 Release the past and be willing to forgive everyone who has hurt you. All that's needed is the willingness. You don't have to do anything more. It has nothing to do with condoning the bad behaviour of others; it has everything to do with not letting yourself be hurt anymore. Let go of the past and move into the present, where **you** have the power in your life.

3 Don't make any conditions about loving yourself. Love yourself now, just the way you are. You are perfect right here and right now. If you wait until you lose weight, or get a better job, or quit smoking, or somebody else loves you first, you may

never do any of those things.

The changes that occur when we accept and love ourselves are always positive. Love is the great power which heals us. It dissolves anger, fear and resentment. So love yourself. Let it flow. Don't block it or refuse it.

When you begin this process of growing, of changing, of loving and supporting your own growth, it doesn't matter where you start. You can begin with the cleansing diet, and it'll lead you into other beneficial areas. You can begin with the mind or the spirit, and they will lead back to the body. It's all one, once you get beyond the superficial. When you begin the process of transforming your life, everything is transformed. It's exactly like cleaning the whole house when it's dirty. Wherever you start, as long as you keep going, it will all eventually be cleaned.

15 *The Home Health Centre*

'It's what you do 95 per cent of the time, not 5 per cent, that matters.'

Natural Health Precept

Natural health practitioners always stress that it's what we do **most** of the time that matters. If we eat a diet high in fats, sugar, salt and refined foods, if we drink too much, if we take unnecessary medications, if we smoke tobacco, it's not possible for a few days of clean living once in a while to undo the damage. Especially if we return to our old self-destructive habits after the break!

Conversely, if we choose to live in a basically healthy and natural way, the odd rich meal or period of unavoidable stress won't do any lasting damage. A practical suggestion made by Leslie Kenton in her book *The Biogenic Diet* is to spend an occasional day just eating fruit, in order to give the body a rest. This practice is particularly valuable if you have been eating 'not wisely but too well'.

She recommends what she calls an 'applefast' at such times, but any fruit you like can be used to give yourself a respite and extra cleansing. Many people abstain from heavy food for a day or two each week or each fortnight, eating fruit or juices. This short period of regular cleansing benefits their overall vitality and sense of well-being enormously.

Really letting yourself rest

If you've been operating at less than your optimum energy and ability, you can plan to provide yourself with an experience of cleansing and healing at home. Choose a time when you have a couple of free days. You might begin by eating a very light diet for two or three days while you're still working or involved in your normal activities. Then, when your free time arrives, you'll be ready to cut back to pure juices or even a day or two on water. During this period, really let yourself rest. Tell your family and friends that you're having a mini-vacation. If you love and respect yourself enough to give yourself this gift, they're likely to respect it too.

During your rest, do the quiet things you love. Write in your journal, read the book you've been wanting to, listen to good music. Sleep and dream as much as you can. This is **your** time; you're recharging your batteries and cleansing yourself at all levels. You're getting to know yourself better. It's **your** life; you don't owe every minute of your time and attention to others.

Every day, use your dry skin brush before having a warm bath or shower. Dry skin brushing encourages lymphatic drainage and breaks down congestion in areas where the lymph flow has become sluggish and toxins have collected. It's particularly beneficial in parts of the body where cellulite has formed, usually in the buttocks and thighs where circulation is poor.

Dry skin brushing improves the circulation, bringing increased nutrients and oxygen to the skin and stimulating the elimination of wastes. The skin is a major organ of elimination and by promoting this function you take some of the load from the liver and kidneys. If you do it regularly, the oil glands function better and make your skin smooth and glowing without the need for oils and lotions.

Don't be too vigorous at first. Brush gently, starting with the soles of the feet, and use long strokes. About a dozen strokes for each body part is enough. Brush in one direction, towart the heart, and avoid any broken or sensitive skin. When you've finished, enjoy your bath or shower.

After two or three days' holiday at your own home health centre, you'll feel revitalised and renewed. You'll be more in tune with yourself, calmer and clearer, and therefore more able to make the choices in your life which benefit you.

Once you decide to do what's right for *you*, you'll discover it's not so hard. Willingness to cooperate with yourself is more than half the battle. The basic principles of a healthy, fulfilling life are not complicated.

Drink pure water and get as much fresh air as you can. Don't poison yourself or your environment with pesticide sprays, air fresheners or other unnecessary commercial concoctions. Take steps to identify the areas of stress in your life and practice deep relaxation on a regular basis. Take appropriate and enjoyable exercise — walking, riding a bicycle, swimming, rebounding on a mini-trampoline, dancing, yoga or properly-designed aerobics are all excellent.

Whole fruit and vegetables

Base most of your diet on fresh, whole fruits and vegetables and eat many of them raw or lightly steamed. You don't need meat to fulfill your protein requirements and maybe this is the time to consider seriously the benefits of reducing or eliminating meat from your diet. The modern methods of raising cattle, sheep, pigs and chickens are often horrific and their flesh contains high levels of hormones, pesticides and other poisons. Their production is also one of the main contributing factors to the overall degradation of the planet.

Even the most dedicated meat-eaters avoid consuming the flesh of other meat-eaters. We don't eat dogs, cats, or other carnivores. But the vegetarian animals which we do eat require ten kilos of pasture for every kilo of meat produced, and the world can no longer afford such waste. The demand for more pasture for cattle, largely to fuel the fast-food industry of the Western world, is directly responsible for the accelerating destruction of our remaining forests. If the land currently supporting herds of cattle was used for grain and leaf crops, we could feed the world's population not only now, but for a long time into the future. The present trend can continue only at the cost of increasing hunger and starvation for more and more people, and of further deterioration of air quality as the forests which absorb carbon dioxide and produce oxygen disappear.

As David Phillips points out, only the fact that more than two-thirds of the world's population is vegetarian is keeping *all of us* from starvation. There is about one half hectare of fertile land on earth for each person, at present. Vegetarians require less than this for their food needs; meat eaters much more. Only about 8 per cent of cultivated crops end up as food for people; the rest is consumed by the animals eaten by a minority of people. The use of vast areas of precious fertile land for grazing animals is an unsustainable pressure on the earth's resources which must be acknowledged and which cannot continue indefinitely.

It's not true that meat provides the only complete dietary source of protein. We need much less protein than most of us eat. Nuts and seeds contain all the essential amino acids, while a proper combination of fruits; vegetables and grains also provides an adequate protein intake. The proteins in plants, grains and seeds are easier to digest than flesh proteins and contain no inherent toxic wastes.

Many people have been convinced that a low-cholesterol diet is necessary, and avoid large amounts of red meat, eggs and dairy products. Some of them have substituted chicken or fish, but there are worryingly high levels of mercury and other toxic wastes in fish, so you should consume it sparingly. Likewise chicken, for unless they are free-ranging, they are fed a chemical diet, of which you're the end consumer.

What about the Pritikin diet? It's basically healthy, but could be improved by a greater focus on fresh fruits, especially in summer and autumn when they are cheap and plentiful.

The simple principles outlined in this book can be your best means of preventing chronic disease, fatigue and feelings of powerlessness. The inner healer, no longer overwhelmed by toxicity, can fulfill its function properly and your spirit and energy can rise to the heights for which they were designed.

Choosing to live well

A wonderful thing begins to happen to us when we make the choice to live well, to eat foods which nourish us and to fulfill our need for productive work, creativity and inner development. The external world not only benefits from our decision but, in turn, responds to us positively. New opportunities arise when we acknowledge our own abilities and make a space for them. People and situations appear which enrich our lives. Creativity — doing what we love — becomes a way of life and brings the greatest possible satisfaction of our deepest needs.

We are all in relationship with each other and with the planet. That relationship improves enormously when we adopt the principles of self-realisation and grow increasingly aware of how each of our actions affects not only ourselves, but the entire ecosystem of which we are a part.

It matters what we do. Each of us, individually, makes a multitude of choices every day which affect both our inner and our outer environment. No matter how many times we may have done things we regret, the point of power is always right *now*. It's never too late to start making the decisions which will strengthen us. And as more and more of us decide to work **with** the positive energies of life and not **against** them, we can make a positive difference in the world.

Sources and Resources

Cleansing and the Cleansing Diet

Airola, Paavo, *Are You Confused?* Health Plus Publishers, 1971.

Airola, Paavo, *Hypoglycemia: A Better Approach*, Health Plus Publishers, 1977.

Diamond, Harvey & Marilyn, *Living Health*, Bantam, 1988.

Hall, Dorothy, *The Natural Health Book*, Nelson, 1976.

Kenton, Leslie, *Ageless Aging*, Century Arrow, 1985.

Kenton, Leslie, *The Biogenic Diet*, Century, 1986.

Phillips, David A., *New Dimensions in Health: From Soil to Psyche*, Angus & Robertson, 1983.

Pritikin, Nathan, *The Pritikin Promise*, Bantam, 1985.

Shelton, Herbert M., *Fasting Can Save Your Life*, Natural Hygiene Press, 1964.

Shelton, Herbert M., *Fasting for Renewal of Life*, Natural Hygiene Press, 1974.

Turchetti, Richard J. & Morella, Joseph J., *New Age Nutrition*, Henry Regnery Co., 1974.

Natural Health (The monthly journal of the Natural Health Society of Australia)

Holistic Health

Capra, Fritjof, *The Turning Point: Science, Society and the Rising Culture*, Simon & Schuster, 1982.

Dychtwald, Ken, *Body/Mind*, Jove Books, 1977.

Goldwag (ed.), Elliott M., *Inner Balance: The Power of Holistic Healing*, Spectrum, 1979.

The New Healers, compiled by The New Dimensions Foundation, And/Or Press, 1980.

162   INNER CLEANSING

Bliss, Shepherd (ed.), *The New Holistic Health Handbook: Living Well in a New Age*, The Stephen Greene Press, 1985.

Pelletier, Kenneth R., *Mind as Healer, Mind as Slayer: A Holistic Approach to Preventing Stress Disorders*, Delta, 1977.

Clinical Ecology, Allergy and Drugs

Cheraskin, Dr E., *Psychodietetics: Food as the Key to Emotional Health*, Bantam, 1974.

Collison, Dr David R., with Timothy Hall, *Why do I Feel so Awful?*, Angus & Robertson, 1989.

Jackson, David M. & Soothill, Rayner, *Is the Medicine Making you Ill?*, The Australian Consumers' Association, Angus & Robertson, 1989.

Mackarness, Dr Richard, *Not All in the Mind*, Pan, 1976.

Diesendorf, Mark (ed.), *The Magic Bullet*, Society for Social Responsibility in Science, 1976.

Personal Transformation

Ellis, Albert & Harper, Robert A., *A New Guide to Rational Living*, Wilshire Book Co., 1975.

Ferguson, Marilyn, *The Aquarian Conspiracy: Personal and Social Transformation in the 1980s.*, J.P. Tarcher, 1980.

Harrison, Dr John, *Love Your Disease: It's Keeping You Healthy*, Angus & Robertson, 1984.

Hay, Louise, *You Can Heal Your Life*, Hay House, 1984.

Gawain, Shakti, *Creative Visualization*, Whatever Publications, Berkeley, 1978.

Mason, L. John, *Guide to Stress Reduction*, Peace Press, 1980.

Meares, Ainslie, *Relief Without Drugs*, Fontana, 1970.

Pelletier, Kenneth R., *Mind as Healer, Mind as Slayer*, Delta, 1977.

Roberts, Jane, *The Nature of Personal Reality*, Prentice-Hall, 1974.

Selye, Hans, *Stress Without Distress*, Hodder & Stoughton, 1974.

Shone, Ronald, *Autohypnosis*, Thorsons Publishers, 1982.

Weekes, Dr Claire, *Self Help For Your Nerves*, Angus & Robertson, 1962.

Other

Burnet, Sir Macfarlane, *Medical Journal of Australia* 2, 1974.

Carson, Rachel, *Silent Spring*, Penguin, 1962.

Grossman, Richard, *The Other Medicines*, Pan, 1986.

Hanssen, Maurice & Marsden, Jill, *The Additive Code Breaker*, Lothian, 1986.

Horne, Ross, *Improving on Pritikin — You can do Better*, Happy Landings, 1988.

Illich, Ivan, *Medical Nemesis — the Expropriation of Health*, Calder & Boyars, London, 1975.

No Kami, Yagyu Tajima, *Zen Swordsman*.

Nolti, Kristine, *My Experience with Living Foods*, Humlegaarden, Denmark.

Pauwels, Louis & Bergier, Jacques, *Morning of the Magicians*, Granada.

Thomas, Lewis, *The Lives of a Cell*, Penguin, 1980.

Your Health Rights: The Essential Guide For Every Australian, Australian Consumers' Association, Australasian Publishing Co., 1988.